A COMPLETE GUIDE
TO
GUNMA PREFECTURE

BEAUTIFUL WORLD ESCAPES
WWW.BEAUTIFULWORLDESCAPES.COM

© Copyright 2017 - All rights reserved.

In no way is it legal to duplicate, copy, or transmit any part of this document in either electronic means or in printed format. Recording of this publication is strictly prohibited and any storage of this document is not allowed unless with written permission from the publisher. All rights reserved.

The information provided herein is stated to be truthful and consistent, in that any liability, in terms of negligence or otherwise, by any usage or abuse of any policies, processes, or directions contained within is the solitary and utter responsibility of the recipient reader. Under no circumstances will any legal responsibility or blame be held against the publisher for any reparation, damages, or monetary loss due to the information herein, either directly or indirectly.

Please note the information contained within this document is for educational and entertainment purposes only. Every attempt has been made to provide accurate, up to date and reliable complete information. No warranties of any kind are expressed or implied. Readers acknowledge that the author is not engaging in the rendering of legal, financial, medical, or professional advice.

Table of Contents

Introduction
Chapter One – Practicalities
Chapter Two – Ikaho Onsen/Haruna Area
Chapter Three – Takasaki
Chapter Four - Kusatsu Area
Chapter Five - Minakami
Chapter Six – Nakanojo
Chapter Seven – Tomioka
Chapter Eight – Katashina-mura
Chapter Nine - Maebashi
Chapter Ten – Useful Phrases
Author Information

Introduction

Only 100 kilometres from Tokyo, magnificent nature and an abundance of hot springs attracts thousands of tourists from all over the world to Gunma Prefecture. Located northwest of the Kanto Plains, visitors flock to the region throughout the year to enjoy the wide range of onsen hot springs, several of which are famous. Kusatsu Onsen is renowned for its hot spring stirring dance known as Yumomi; Minakami Onsen boasts high quality services and a range of outdoor activities; Shima Onsen is nestled in a quiet mountainous region, ideal for those seeking peace and relaxation; and the Stone Steps makes Ikaho Onsen famous.

Situated in the heart of Honshu, the main island that makes up Japan, the shape of Gunma Prefecture resembles a crane flapping in the wind. As such, it is referred to as *Gunma Prefecture with the shape of a soaring crane*' within a popular local card game. It boasts a wide range of natural features, from tall imposing mountains to fat plains and dense forests. The Tone River originates in Gunma Prefecture, having the widest basin area in the country. The region is also known as Tokyo's Water Tank, due to the many forests which act as natural dams (along with manmade ones). With clean water and abundant greenery, its beautiful scenery delights the senses.

Ozegahara, an elevated marshland, is one of Gunma Prefecture's top scenic spots, bordering along the borders with Tochigi, Fukushima, and Niigata Prefectures. Other scenic sights not to miss includes Yugama, a crater lake on Mount Kusatasu-Shirane-san boasting emerald green waters; Watarase Valley, where the best views over the valley can be enjoyed from a slow sightseeing train; and Mount Tanigawa-dake, where visitors are carried to the top via cable car.

For history and culture lovers, Gunma Prefectures offers a wealth of attractions to enjoy. Kofun, groups of ancient burial mounds, can be found throughout the region, with the Yawata, Shiroishi, and Hotoda Burial Mounds being the most popular. They showcase the rich culture that flourished here thousands of years ago. Historical shrines and temples such as Serada Toshogu, Haruna Shrine, and Myogi Shrine are particularly popular with tourists, especially Haruna Shrine, which is said to be a spiritual power hotspot. The establishment of the Tomioka Silk Mill in 1872, as well as the three related sites of Arafune Cold Storage, Takayama-sha Sericulture School, and Tajima Yahei Sericulture Farm allowed the region to prosper with the mass production of raw silk, exporting high quality silk products throughout the world. These four sites were designated a World Heritage Site in 2014.

The long periods of sunshine throughout the year have allowed Gunma Prefecture to produce many varieties of produce. These include grains, dairy products, fruits, vegetables, pork, and beef, exporting them to many places around the country, such as Tokyo. Visitors to Gunma Prefecture will discover many regional specialties to enjoy, from sophisticated dishes to the more budget conscious, but all designed to please the palette.

Chapter One – Practicalities

Getting to Gunma

By Aeroplane

The nearest international airports to Gunma Prefecture are Matsumoto Airport (MMJ) and Tokyo Haneda International Airport (RJTT), located 105.31 kilometres and 112.51 kilometres away from Maebashi, the prefectural capital.

Taxis, long-distance buses, and trains are available outside both airports, making it easy to reach the major cities and popular towns in Gunma Prefecture.

By Train

The easiest way to reach Gunma Prefecture from Matsumoto and Haneda Airports is via train. The JR East has eight lines throughout the prefecture, with a shinkansen, or bullet train, taking only 50 minutes from Tokyo. The Joetsu Shinkansen is a fast-speed train that connects Tokyo and Niigata Prefecture by way of the Tohoku Shinansen, stopping at the Jomo-Kogen Station in the town of Minakami in Gunma Prefecture. The Horuriku Shinkansen, connecting Tokyo with Kanazawa Prefecture, stops at Takasaki and Annaka-Haruna. The Takasaki Line operates between Omiya Station in Saitama Prefecture with Takasaki Station in Gunma Prefecture and also operated by the JR East Company and was the first privately built railway in the country.

Four additional railways operate in Gunma Prefecture. The Tobu Railway runs four lines of their own, including the Tobu Isesaki Line, which runs from Tobu-Dobutsu-Koen Station in Saitama Prefecture to Isesaki Station in Gunma Prefecture. The Tobu Sano Line operates between Tatebayashi Station in Gunma Prefecture and Kuzo Station in Sano, Tochigi Prefecture.

The Joshin Electric Railway operates between Takasaki Station and Shimonita Station in Gunma Prefecture, which also owns several buses. The Jomo Electric Railway Company stops at 22 stations throughout the prefecture, covering a total distance of 25.4 kilometres. The Wakarase Keikoku Railway has one line operating in Gunma and Tochigi Prefecture, purchased from the JR East Company in 1989, and stops at 17 stations.

By Long Distance Bus

Long distance buses can be found outside many places within Gunma Prefecture, along with the major airports such as Tokyo Haneda Airport and Narita Airport. The prices for long distance buses are much cheaper than the train or shinkansen, but they do take longer to reach their destination. It takes around two and a half hours from Tokyo to Gunma Prefecture via the Tohoku Expressway depending on the traffic.

Getting Around Gunma Prefecture

Most of the cities and towns in Gunma Prefecture have their own local bus networks that stop outside many of the bigger attractions. Maps, timetables, and fares can be found at the travel centres in the bigger cities and tourist destinations.

Climate

The weather in Gunma Prefecture varies due to its diverse geography. In the mountainous regions the weather can be cold even in the spring and summer, and the higher elevations can experience a great amount of snow during the winter. In the lower elevations, the prefecture is known for the *karakkaze*, a bitterly dry and cold wind that blows through the region when the snow falls on the coastline of Niigata. The average temperature in Maebashi, the prefectural capital, is 18°C (64.4°F) in April, and 30.1°C (86.2°F) in August, although temperatures can rise as high as 39.1°C (102.4°F) in the summer. The coldest month in Maebashi is -1.8°C (28.8°F) in January, although it can drop as low as -11.8°C (10.8°F), with an average snowfall of 6.5 inches. The rainy season lasts between June and September.

It is recommended that visitors to Gunma Prefecture always pack suitable clothing for the season. The prefecture is known for being one of the sunniest destinations in the country, so sunscreen and other protection from the sun is recommended throughout the year. Light clothing and layers are recommended for the summer, along with hats, lip balm, sunglasses, hats, and an umbrella. Thick gloves, scarves, hats, warm socks, waterproof footwear, and a thick jacket are necessities for visiting in the winter.

Currency

The currency used in Japan is the Japanese Yen (JYP), with the symbol being the ¥. As of this guide being published, the currency rates are as follows:

1 JYP = £0.006, $0.008

10 JYP = £0.06, $0.08

100 JYP = £0.67, $0.84

1,000 JYP = $6.79, $8.48

10,000 = £67.90, $84.81

100,000 = £679.02, £848.10

International dialling code

81

Time zone

UTC/GMT +9 hours

Wi-Fi

Internet service is fast, reliable, and safe in Japan. Recently, the government and local businesses have started offering free Wi-Fi networks for international visitors to use, the most of which can be found in and around airports, railway stations, and certain coffee shops and convenience stores. The networks vary; some are easy to connect whilst others require a more detailed registration form. Paid Wi-Fi spots are more frequent than the free ones, offering a range of plans. Most of these are on a daily or weekly basis, with one-day passes costing around ¥500 – 800. Registration forms are mainly in Japanese and some require a Japanese bank account or address. Wi200 300, Docomo Wi-Fi for Visitor, and SoftBank Wi-Fi Spot (EX) offer registration forms in English and accept foreign credit cards. Alternatively, there are several companies that rent smartphones which include unlimited data and Wi-Fi tethering, allowing them to act as local hotspots. International roaming is another alternative but is only available if your phone works in Japan and your provider has an agreement with a Japanese provider. Please note that this is quite an expensive option. Internet cafes, also known as netto cafes and manga cafes, rent computers connected to the internet for a few hundred yen an hour. Some require a registration fee, and most are situated around the train stations. Most hotels will offer free internet in their guest rooms via a wireless network. Ryokans, traditional Japanese guesthouses, do not offer free internet in their rooms; some will have a shared computer room or may not provide any at all.

Plug type

Type A North American/Japanese 2 blade and type B American 3-pin

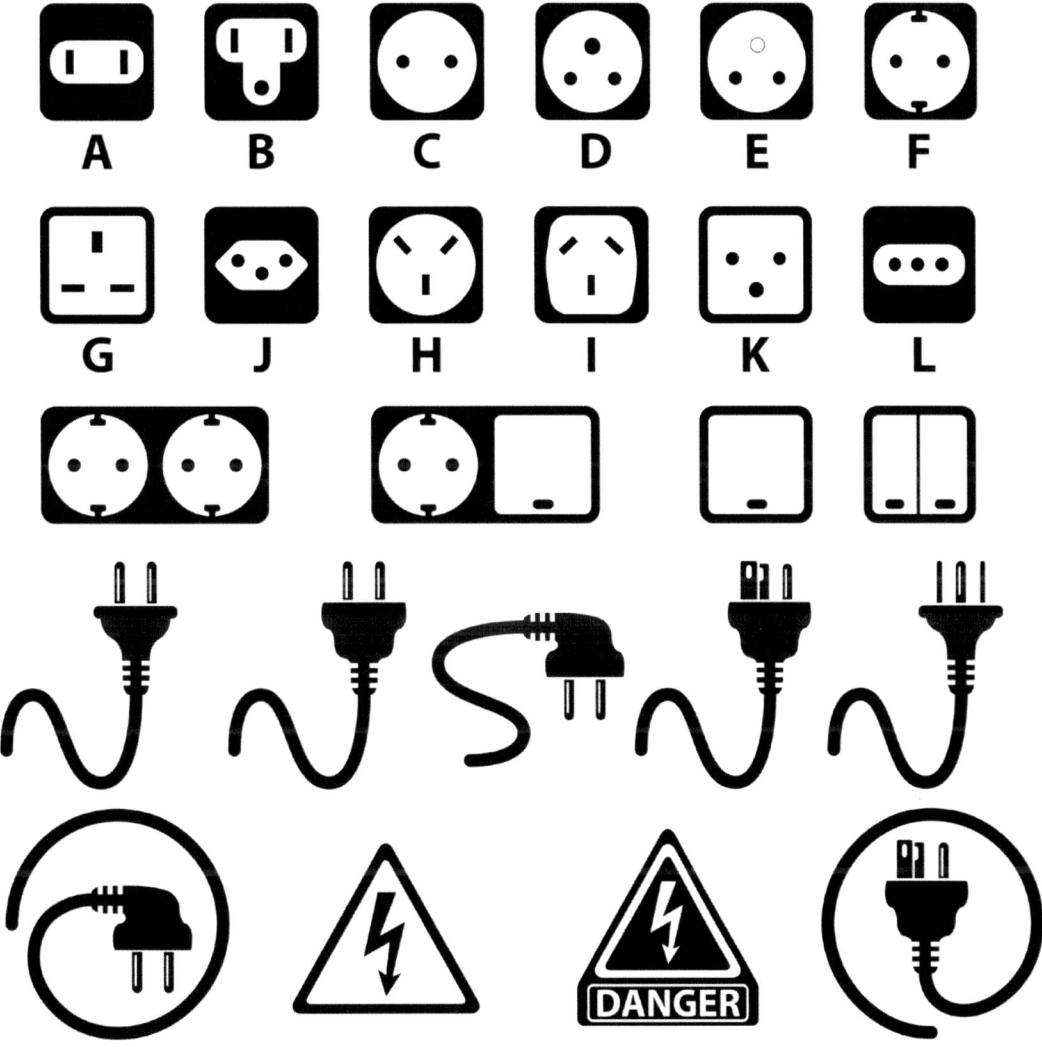

Banks

ATMs, banks, and moneychangers can be found throughout Japan, although working hours tend to be restrictive with banks operating between 09:00 – 15:00 Monday to Friday. Most Japanese banks do not close at lunchtime and ATMs are open for longer hours, opening until 19:00 on week days and 17:00 on weekends and public holidays. Citibank Japan (now SMBC Trust Bank) was the first Japanese bank to offer 24-hour ATMs in Tokyo, Osaka, Kobe, Nagoya, Kyoto, Yokohama, Saitama and several other larger cities where you can use Citibank cards issued in your countries to access money. Some banks will charge for ATM withdrawals depending on the day and time. Japan is still a mostly cash-only country and it is recommended that traveller's carry more cash on hand than what you may do at home. Traveller's cheques can be exchanged at most banks, but not exchanged for goods or services. English-speaking Bureau de Change can be found at most airports, including Narita Airport. Hotels, large shopping centres and department stores will accept most credit cards; most restaurants, cafes, and smaller stores will only accept cash.

Smoking

Smoking is legal in Japan, although the government is trying to raise awareness of health issues. Limited indoor bans have been implemented in certain areas such as Kanagawa and Hyogo

Prefectures, but not nationally. Particular areas in Tokyo have started implementing smoking bans, including busy streets. Several international businesses, such as Starbucks, McDonalds, and Kentucky Fried Chicken have banned smoking in their establishments. Cigarettes can be purchased throughout the country, with vending machines offering easy access. It is illegal to sell cigarettes to anyone under the age of 20.

Driving

With excellent public transportation, most people do not rely on cars to get around the bigger cities such as Tokyo, Osaka, Yokohama, and Kyoto. However, transportation outside these cities are much more infrequent and unreliable, making cars a necessity. Cars drive on the left-hand side in Japan with the driver's seat and steering wheel on the right-hand side of the vehicle. Drivers are required to be at least 18 years old and foreign drivers are permitted to drive in Japan with an International Driving Permit (IDP). These must be obtained in your home countries as they cannot be issued in Japan. Most signs are displayed in both Japanese and English. Driving whilst intoxicated is illegal. Conditions of most Japanese roads is considered good, although the roads can get slippery or hard to manoeuvre when heavy snow falls. The biggest dangers tend to be from cyclists cycling in the wrong lane or from those stopping their vehicles that block traffic.

Tipping

Tipping is not the norm in Japan and it is not customary to leave a tip in restaurants, cafes, bars, or taxis; if insisted, it could cause embarrassment or confusion. A polite thank you and a warm smile is more appreciated.

Emergency numbers

Police – 110, Coast Guard – 118, Fire, Ambulance, and Emergency rescue – 119

Haggling

Haggling is not accepted in most places in Japan, especially at larger shops and department stores. Haggling can be done at flea markets; be polite and let it come naturally instead of forced.

Public Holidays

New Year's Day – 1st January (元日 *Ganjitsu*)

Coming of Age Day – Second Monday of January (成人の日 *Seijin no Hi*)

National Foundation Day – 11th February (建国記念の日 *Kenkoku Kinen no Hi*)

Vernal Equinox – around 20th March (春分の日 *Shunbun no Hi*)

Showa Day – 29th April (昭和の日 *Shōwa no Hi*)

Constitutional Day – 3rd May (憲法記念日 *Kenpō Kinenbi*)

Greenery Day – 4th May (みどりの日 *Midori no Hi*)

Children's Day – 5th May (こどもの日 *Kodomo no Hi*)

Marine Day – Third Monday of July (海の日 *Umi no Hi*)

Mountain Day – 11th August (山の日 *Yama no Hi*)

Respect for the Aged Day – Third Monday of September (敬老の日 *Keirō no Hi*)

Autumnal Equinox Day – Around 23rd September (秋分の日 *Shūbun no Hi*)

Health and Sports Day – Second Monday of October (体育の日 *Taiiku no Hi*)

Culture Day – 3rd November (文化の日 *Bunka no Hi*)

Labour Thanksgiving Day – 23rd November (勤労感謝の日 *Kinrō Kansha no Hi*)

The Emperor's Birthday – 23rd December (天皇誕生日 *Tennō Tanjōbi*)

Visas

Most visitors are issued with a 90-day visa upon arrival that cannot be extended in Japan. Visitors from certain countries can have their 90-day visa extended for another 90 days whilst in Japan. Other nationalities are issued with a 15-day waiver. Visitors from the following countries are issued with a 90-day visa upon arrival: Australia, Canada, France, Hong Kong, Ireland, Israel, Italy, Malaysia, Netherlands, New Zealand, the Republic of Korea, Singapore, Spain, Taiwan, USA. Visitors from the following countries are issued with a 90-day visa which can be extended for another 90 days whilst in Japan: Austria, Germany, Ireland, Mexico, Switzerland, the United Kingdom. Those who wish to extend their visa in Japan should apply at the Osaka Immigration Bureau Kyoto Branch, located on the fourth floor of the Dai Ni Chiho Godochosha Building at 34-12 Higashi Marutamachi, Kawabata Higashi-iru, Sakyo-ku. Visitors from Brunei and Thailand are issued with a 15-day visa upon arrival. Visitors from all other countries should check with their local Japanese embassy before arriving.

Embassies in Japan

British Embassy
1 Ichiban-cho, Chiyoda-ku, Tokyo.
Phone: (+81) 3 5211-1100
Fax: (+81) 3 5275-3164
Website: https://www.contact-embassy.service.gov.uk/?country=Japan&post=British%20Embassy%20Tokyo
Email: public-enquiries.tokyo@fco.gov.uk
Opening Hours: The British Embassy is open Monday to Friday 09:30 - 16:30. The Consular section is open Tuesday 09:30 - 12:00, 14:00 - 17:00. Friday 09:30 - 13:00. Closed on Mondays, Wednesdays and Thursdays. (Please note: appointments required for all documentary and notarial services)

U.S. Embassy

1-10-5 Akasaka Minato-ku, Tokyo 107-8420.
Phone: (+81) 3 3224-5000
Fax: (+81) 3 3505-1862
Website: http://tokyo.usembassy.gov
Opening Hours: Monday to Friday from 08:30 - 12:30, 14:00 to 16:00. Closed on holidays.

Embassy of Spain
1-3-29, Roppongi Minato-ku, Tokyo 106-0032
Phone (+81) 3 3583-8532 / 1
Fax (+81) 3 3582-8627
Email: embespjp@mail.mae.es

Embassy of the Federal Republic of Yugoslavia
4-7-24, Kitashinagawa, Shinagawa-ku, Tokyo 140-0001
Phone: (+81) 3 3447-35-71
Fax: (+81) 3 3447-3573
Website: http://www.serbianembassy.jp
Email: embassy@serbianembassy.jp
Opening Hours: Embassy: 09:00 - 12:00; 13:00 - 17:00 (prior appointment required). Consular Section: 10:00 - 12:00 (prior appointment required)

Embassy of the Slovak Republic
2-16-14 Hiroo Shibuya-ku Japan
Phone: (+81) 3 3400 8122
Fax: (+81-3) 3406 6215
Website: http://www.mzv.sk/Tokyo
Email: emb.tokyo@mzv.sk

Embassy of Romania
106-0031 Tokyo-to, Minato-ku Nishi-Azabu, 3-16-19 Tokyo
Phone: ++ (81) 3 34790311
Fax: ++ (81) 3 34790312

Embassy of New Zealand
20-40 Kamiyama-cho Shibuya-ku 150-0047
Phone: +81 3 3467 2271
Fax: +81 3 3467 6843
Website: http://www.nzembassy.com/home.cfm?c=17
Email: nzemb.tky@mail.com
Opening Hours: Monday (closed) -Tuesday – Thursday, Friday 09.00 - 13.00, 09.00 - 12.00

Mexican Embassy
2-15-1, Nagata-cho Chiyoda-Ku Tokyo 100-0014
Phone (+81) 3 3581 1131; (+81) 3 3581 1135
Fax (+81) 3 3581 4058
Website: http://embamex.sre.gob.mx/japon/
Email: embajadamexicojapon@sre.gob.mx

Mongolian Embassy
21-4 Kamiyama Cho Shibuya Ku, Tokyo 150-0047
Phone: (+81) 3 3469-2088
Fax (+81) 3 3469-2216
Website: http://www.tokyo.mfa.gov.mn/
Email: embassy.tokyo@yahoo.com

Embassy of Argentina
2-14-14 Moto Azabu, Minato-ku, Tokyo 106-0046
Phone: ++81 3 54207101/ ++ 81 3 54207102
Website: http://ejapo.cancilleria.gov.ar/
Email: ejapo@cancilleria.gob.ar
Opening Hours: 09:00 - 18:00

Australian Embassy
2-1-14 Mita Minato-Ku Tokyo 108-8361
Phone: +(81) 3 5232-4111
Fax +(81) 3 5232 4149
Website: http://www.australia.or.jp/en/
Email: auscitzreg.tokyo@dfat.gov.au
Opening Hours: Monday to Friday 09:00 - 12:30 and 13:30 - 17:00

Embassy of Ecuador
Kowa Building, Room 806 4-12-24 Nishi-Azabu Minato-Ku, Tokyo 106-0031
Phone: (+81) 3 3499 2800 / (+81) 3 3499 2866
Fax: (+81) 3 3499 4400
Website: http://www.ecuador-embassy.or.jp/
Email: eecujapon@mmrree.gob.ec, info@ecuador-embassy.or.jp
Opening Hours: 09:30 - 18:00

Embassy of Pakistan
4-6-17, Minami-Azabu, Minato-Ku, Tokyo 106-0047
Phone: (+81) 3-5421-7741-42
Fax: (+81) 3-5421-3610
Website: http://www.pakistanembassyjapan.com
Email: info@pakistanembassyjapan.com, pareptokyo@hotmail.com

Embassy of Paraguay
Ichibancho TG Building. Nr. 2, 7F 2-2 Ichibancho Chiyoda-ku, Tokyo 102-0082
Phone: +(81) 3 3265-5271
Fax: +(81) 3 3265-5273
Website: http://www.embapar.jp/
Email: japonembaparsc@mre.gov.py
Opening Hours: Monday to Thursday 10:00 - 17:00

Embassy of Portugal
Olympia Annex No. 304/6, 31-21 Jingumae 6-chome, Shibuya-ku, Tokyo 150
Phone: (+81) 3 34007907/8
Fax: (+81) 3 34007909
Website: http://www.pnsnet.co.jp/users/cltembpt

Embassy of Venezuela
No. 38 Kowa Building, Rm. 703 12-24 Nishi Azabu 4-Chome Minato-ku 106-0031 Tokyo,
Phone: (+81) 3 3409 1501
Fax: (+81) 3 3409 1505
Website: http://www.venezuela.or.jp
Email: embavene@interlink.or.jp
Opening Hours: 09:00 to 17:00

Embassy of India
2-2-11 Kudan-Minami Chiyoda-ku, Tokyo 102-0074
Phone: (81) 3 3262-2391 to 97
Fax: (81) 3 3234-4866
Website: https://www.indembassy-tokyo.gov.in/
Email: amboffice.tokyo@mea.gov.in

Embassy of Hungary
2-17-14 Mita, Minato-ku, Tokyo 108-0073
Phone: (+81) 3 3798-8801/4
Fax: (+81) 3 3798-8812
Website: http://www.mfa.gov.hu/emb/tokyo
Email: huembtio@gol.com
Opening Hours: Monday – Friday 8:30 - 17:00, Friday 8:30 - 14:30

Embassy of Finland
3-5-39, Minami-Azabu, Minato-ku, Tokyo 106-8561
Phone: (+81) 3 5447 6000
Fax: (+81) 3 5447 6042
Website: http://www.finland.or.jp/
Email: sanomat.tok@formin.fi
Opening Hours: Monday - Friday 09.00 - 12.00, 13.00 - 17.15

Embassy of France
11-11-14 Minami Azabu Minato-Ku Tokyo 106-0047
Phone: (+81) 3 57 98 60 00
Fax: (+81) 3 57 98 62 06 / 57 98 62 12
Website: http://www.ambafrance-jp.org

Embassy of Vietnam
50-11, Motoyoyogi-cho Shibuya-ku Tokyo 151
Phone: (+81) 3 3466 3311
Fax: (+81)3 3466 3391; 3466 7652; 3466 3312
Website: http://www.mofa.gov.vn/vnemb.jp/
Email: vnembasy@blue.ocn.ne.jp

Embassy of The Republic of Korea
4-4-10, Yotsuya Shinjuku-ku Tokyo 160-0004
Phone: (+81) 3 3452-7611 / 9
Fax: (+81) 3 5232-6911

Embassy of Ireland
Ireland House 5F 2-10-7 Kojimachi Chiyoda-Ku, Tokyo 102-0083
Phone: (+81) 3 3263-0695
Fax: (+81) 3 3265-2275
Website: http://www.embassyofireland.jp/
Opening Hours: Public Hours: 10:00 - 12.30, 14:00 - 16:00. Visa Hours: Wednesdays only 14:00 - 16:00

Embassy of the Philippines
5-15-5 Roppongi Minato-ku, Tokyo 106-8537
Phone: (+81) 3 5562-1600
Fax: (+81) 3 5562-1603
Website: http://tokyo.philembassy.net
Email: phjp@gol.com, info@philembassy.net
Opening Hours: Monday to Friday 09:00 – 18:00

Embassy of Singapore
5-12-3, Roppongi Minato-ku Tokyo 106-0032
Phone: (+81) 3 3586 9111
Fax: (+81) 3 3582 1085
Website: http://www.mfa.gov.sg/tokyo
Email: singemb@gol.com
Opening Hours: Monday to Friday 09:00 - 12.30, 13:30 – 17:30. Consular Services: Monday to Friday 09:30 - 12.00, 14:00 – 17:00pm

Embassy of South Africa
Oriken Hirakawacho building 3rd and 4th Floor 2-1-1 Hirakawa-cho Chiyoda-ku 102-0093 Tokyo
Phone: (+81) 3 3265-3366
Fax: (+81) 3 3265-1108
Website: http://www.sajapan.org
Email: visa@rsatk.com
Opening Hours: Monday to Friday 09:00 12:00

Embassy of Canada
7- 3-38 Akasaka,Minato-ku Tokyo 107-8503
Phone: (+81) 3 5412-6200
Fax: (+81) 3 5412-6289
Website: http://www.canadainternational.gc.ca/japan-japon/index.aspx?lang=eng
Email: tokyo-cs@international.gc.ca
Opening Hours: Monday to Friday 09:00 - 17:30

Royal Thai Embassy
3-14-6, Kami-Osaki, Shinagawa-ku Tokyo 141-0021
Phone: (+81) 3 5789-2433
Fax: (+81) 3 5789-2428
Website: http://www.thaiembassy.jp/, http://www.thaiembassy.jp/
Email: infosect@thaiembassy.jp

Opening Hours: Monday to Friday VISA Application 09:00 – 11:45, Collection 13:30 – 15:00 Certification 09:00 – 11:45, Thai Passport 09:00 – 11:30, 13: 30 – 14:30, Registration 09:00 – 11:30, 13:30 – 14:30, Birth Certificate 09:00 - 11.30, 13:30 – 14:30

Embassy of Malaysia
20-16, Nanpeidai-cho Shibuya-ku, Tokyo 150-0036
Phone: (+81) 3 3476-3840
Fax: (+81) 3 3476-4971
Website: http://www.kln.gov.my/perwakilan/tokyo
Email: mwtokyo.kln@1govuc.gov.my
Opening Hours: Monday to Friday 9:00 - 12:30, 13:30 - 17:00

Embassy of Italy
2-5-4 Mita, Minato-ku Tokyo 108-8302
Phone: (+81) 3 3453 5291
Fax: (+81) 3 57652918
Website: http://www.ambtokyo.esteri.it
Email: ambasciata.tokyo@esteri.it

Embassy of Sweden
1-10-3-100 Roppongi Minato-ku Tokyo 106-0032 Japan
Phone: (+81) 3 5562 5050
Fax: (+81) 3 5562 90 95
Email: ambassaden.tokyo@gov.se
Opening Hours: Monday to Friday 09.00 - 12.30, 13.30 - 17.30

Embassy of Indonesia
5-2-9 Highashi-Gotanda Shinagawa-ku Tokyo 141-0022
Phone: (+81) 3 3441-4201
Fax: (+81)3 3447-1697
Website: http://www.indonesian-embassy.jp
Email: indonembsatu@hpo.net

Embassy of Israel
3 Nibancho, Chiyoda-ku 102-0084 Tokyo
Phone: (+81) 3 32640911
Fax: (+81) 3 32640832
Website: http://tokyo.mfa.gov.il
Email: info@tokyo.mfa.gov.il
Opening Hours: Monday to Thursday 09:00 - 17:30, Friday 09:00 - 15:15

Embassy of Russia
1-1, Azabudai; 2-chome, Minato-ku, Tokyo, 106-004
Phone: (+81) 3 3583-4224, 3583-5982, 3583-4297
Fax: (+81) 3 3505-0593
Website: http://www.japan.mid.ru/
Email: rosconsl@ma.kcom.ne.jp

Royal Danish Embassy
29-6 Sarugaku-cho Shibuya-ku Tokyo 150-0033

Phone: (+81) 3 3496 3001
Fax: (+81) 3 3496 3440
Website: http://www.ambtokyo.um.dk
Email: tyoamb@um.dk
Opening Hours: Monday to Friday 9:30 - 12:00, 13:00 pm - 17:30

Embassy of Belgium
Nibancho 5-4 Chiyoda-ku Tokyo 102-0084
Phone: (+81) 3 326 201 91
Fax: (+81) 3 326 206 51, +81 3 326 202 31
Website: http://www.diplomatie.be/tokyo/
Email: tokyo@diplobel.fed.be
Opening Hours: Monday to Wednesday 09:30 - 12:30, 13:30 - 17:30. Thursday - Friday 09:30 - 12:30

Chinese Embassy
3-4-33 Moto-Azabu Minato-Ku, Tokyo
Phone: (+81) 3 34033388
Fax: (+81) 3 34033345
Website: http://www.china-embassy.or.jp
Email: lsb@china-embassy.or.jp

Royal Norwegian Embassy
5-12-2 Minami Azabu, Minato-ku, Tokyo, 106-0047
Phone: (+81) 3 6408-8100
Fax: (+81) 3 6408-8199
Website: http://www.norway.or.jp/Embassy/english/
Email: emb.tokyo@mfa.no

Embassy of Switzerland
5-9-12 Minami-Azabu Minato-ku Tokyo 106-8589
Phone: (+81) 3 3473 01 21, (+81) 3 3473 01 30
Fax: (+81) 3 3473 60 90
Website: http://www.eda.admin.ch/tokyo
Email: tok.vertretung@eda.admin.ch

Osaka

Consulate General of the Republic of Korea

2-3-4 Nishi-Shimsaibashi Chuo-ku Osaka
Phone: (+81) 6-6213-1401 / 5

Chinese Consulate General
3-9-2 Utsubohonmach, Nishiku Osaka, 550
Phone: (+81) 6 64459481, (+81) 6 64459482
Fax: (+81) 6 64459475 (+81) 6 64459480
Website: http://osaka.china-consulate.org
Email: chinaconsul_osa_jp@mfa.gov.cn

Australian Consulate General

Twin 21 MID Tower, 16th Floor 2-1-61, Shiromi, Chuo-ku Osaka 540-6126
Phone: +81 6 6941-9271, +81 6-6941-9448
Fax: +81 6 6920-4543
Website: http://www.australia.or.jp/en/consular/osaka/
Email: http:www.australia.or.jp/enconsularosakaenquiry.php

Consulate General of United States
2-11-5, Nishitenma Kita-ku, Osaka 530-8543
Phone: (+81) 6 6315-5900
Website: http://osaka.usconsulate.gov

Philippine Consulate General
Twin 21 MID Tower 24F 2-1-61 Shiromi, Chuo-Ku, Osaka 540-6124 Japan
Phone: (+81) 6 6910-7881
Fax: (+81) 6 6910-8734
Email: osakapc@osk.3web.ne.jp
Opening Hours: 09:00 - 17:00

Consulate of Thailand
No. 9 No. 16 Bangkok Bank Building, 4th Floor Osaka Kyutaro-cho 1-chome Yubinbango541-0056, Chuo-ku, Osaka
Phone: (+81) 6 6262-9226, 6 6262-92267
Fax: (+81) 6 6262-9228
Website: http://www.thaiconsulate.jp/
Email: rtcg-osk@jupiter.plala.or.jp
Opening Hours: 09:30 - 12:30, 13:30 - 17:30

Nagoya

Consulate General of the Republic of Korea

1-19-12, Meieki-minami Nakamura-ku 450-0003 Nagoya
Phone: (+81) 52-586-9221 / 6

Consulate of United States
Nagoya International Centre Building. 6F 1-47-1 Nagono, Nakamura-ku Nagoya 450-0001
Phone: (+81) 52 581-4501
Fax: (+81) 52 6-6315-5914
Website: http://nagoya.usconsulate.gov
Email: AOK@state.gov
Opening Hours: Monday to Friday 08:30 - 17:30

Sri Lankan Consulate General
3-1-36 Noritake shin-Mach Nishi-ku, Nagoya 451-8501
Phone :(+81) 52-261-7123
Fax: (+81) 52-561-4051

Consulate General of the Republic of Korea

1-1-3, Jigyohama Chuo-ku 810-0065 Fukuoka
Phone: (+81) 92-771-0461

Consulate General of the Republic of Korea
2-21-5 Nakayamate-Dori Chuo-Ku, Kobe
Phone: (+81) 78-221-4853 / 5

Australian Consulate-General
7th Floor Tenjin Twin Building 1-6-8 Tenjin, Chuo-ku Fukuoka City 810-0001
Phone: (+81) 92 734 5055
Fax: (+81) 92 734 5058
Website: http://www.australia.or.jp/en/consular/fukuoka/
Opening Hours: Monday to Friday 09:00 - 17:30

Australian Consulate
17th Floor, Sapporo Centre Building North 5, West 6-2, Chuo-ku 060-0005 Sapporo
Phone: (+81) 011-242-4381
Fax: (+81) 011-242-4383
Website: http://www.australia.or.jp/en/consular/sapporo/
Opening Hours: Tuesday and Thursday 09:00 - 17:00

Consulate General of United States
Kita 1-Jo Nishi 28-Chome, Chuo-Ku Sapporo 064-0821
Phone: (+81) 11 641-1115
Fax: (+81) 11 643-1283
Website: http://sapporo.usconsulate.gov
Opening Hours: 09:00 – 12:00, 13:00 – 15:00

Consulate General of United States
2-1-1 Toyama Urasoe City, Okinawa
Phone: (+81) 98 876-4211
Fax: (+81) 98 876-4243
Website: http://naha.usconsulate.gov
Email: NahaACS@state.gov
Opening Hours: Monday to Thursday 08:00 - 11:30, 13:00 – 15:00

Consulate of Philippines
2nd Floor Aljon Building Naha City, Okinawa 901-22
Phone: (+81) 98 892-5486
Fax: (+81) 98 892-5487

Consulate of Philippines in Sapporo
1-2-27 Ichijo Nishi Hakken Nishi-Ku Sapporo-shi 063
Phone: (+81) 12 386-2026
Fax: (+81) 11 611-2225

Consulate of United States
5-26 Ohori 2-chome, Chuo-ku Fukuoka 810-0052
Phone: (+81) 92 751-9331
Website: http://fukuoka.usconsulate.gov

Opening Hours: Monday - Friday 08:45 - 17:30

Recommended Vaccinations:

Visitors to Japan should take an International Certificate of Vaccination (also known as the yellow booklet) which lists the vaccinations you have received. The World Health Organization (WHO) recommends that visitors to Japan should have the following vaccinations:

Hepatitis A
Hepatitis B
Japanese Encephalitis
Measles, Mumps, and Rubella (MMR)
Rabies

Travelling with children:

Japan is considered a safe country to explore with children. The country is particularly clean, easy to get around, and has plenty of mod cons. The larger cities have plenty of toilets and baby changing facilities. Breastfeeding is not particularly done in public, however there are plenty of nursing stations in shopping malls, department stores, and larger train stations. It may be hard to get on a busy train during the morning rush hour (07:30 – 09:00) with a pram, but children under 12 years old can travel with mothers in the women-only carriages.

Grocery stores and pharmacies will sell baby food and formula; nappies/diapers and baby wipes can also be found in pharmacies. For fussy eaters, it is recommended that you bring a few snacks your little ones prefer as the selection of foreign foods in Japan is not extensive. It might be a good idea to pack small plastic knives, forks, and spoons for dining out if your child is not comfortable using chopsticks. Any medicines your child may need should be brought with you as most Japanese pharmacies do not stock foreign brands. If you are planning on travelling throughout the country, it might be worthwhile bringing anti-motion sickness medication.

Female travellers

Japan is considered a safe country for women to travel to, although crimes against women are believed to be under-reported. Local women tend not to wear low-cut clothing or items that draw attention to themselves. Some foreign women have reported of prying questions or verbal harassment, especially around bars and nightclubs. There are women only carriages on trains for women to get away from *chikan*, men who grope women on busy trains. It is advised that female travellers take the same safety precautions they would normally do in their home countries.

LGBT

Homosexually is legal in Japan, although it is not flaunted about. Sexuality is considered a private matter in Japan and whether one is homosexual or heterosexual, is not flaunted in public. Local gay life is inaccessible for visitors, and even harder for lesbians who are, for the most part, invisible. However, Japan is starting to see a market for gay travel and many homosexual visitors have claimed they had no issues with locals. Whilst there are hundreds of gay bars in Tokyo, only a few allow foreigners.

Disabilities

Japan has implemented a law that ensures many places are accessible for those with disabilities. On first glance, some attractions, including UNESCO World Heritage sites and National Historic sites, may not appear to be accessible for wheelchairs but have a not-so-obvious side door, gate, or an elevator hidden in a building resembling a temple. However, there are some sites, such as temples and shrines located on top of hills and mountains, that may not have any access for those with disabilities. Travelling on public transportation is easy; after purchasing your ticket, the seller will arrange for you to get on the train and contact the station you are getting off at to help you off with a portable ramp. Disabled toilets, known locally as multi-purpose toilets, are located near the standard men's and women's toilets in hotels, train stations, restaurants, and department stores. They feature extra-wide space, sinks for cleaning ostomate bags, and handrails, as well as baby changing facilities. Please note, however, these toilets are not regulated and no two are the same. Most hotel rooms vary with their disability-related amenities, but most ryokans are not disability-friendly.

Chapter Two – Ikaho Onsen/Haruna Area

Located within Kitagunma District, Ikaho was a small town boasting a population of almost 4,000 residents, but was merged into Shibukawa city in 2005 along with four additional villages. It is famous for the Ikaho Onsen, a hot spring resort situated on the north-eastern foot of Mount Haruna-san, between 720 – 820 meters above sea level. Believed to have been established in the seventh century, the waters are rich in carbonic acid and sulphate, with concentrations high enough to occasionally dye towels red. Kaijika Bridge, located nearby, offers panoramic views of the surrounding forest which is especially beautiful in autumn when the leaves transform into brilliant shades of red.

Mount Haruna-san is part of the Jomo Sanzan, also known as the Three Famous Mountains in Gunma Prefecture, along with Mount Akagi-yama and Amount Myogi-san. The dual volcano boasts a flat caldera (a large cauldron-like depression that forms after magma has burst out from its chamber), along with other scenic spots, including Haruna Fuji and Lake Haruna-ko, the latter of which is popular with for hikers and cyclists.

Shibukawa offers a variety of historical and cultural attractions to explore, including the Stone Steps. Consisting of 365 stone steps that heads from Ikaho Shrine towards the town, the various souvenir stores and other facilities established along either side makes it a popular attraction.

Ikaho Onsen

Ikaho is famous for its hot spring resorts, which boast high concentrations of iron. As a result, the waters are a usual reddish-brown colour and has a metallic taste. It is said that whoever drinks or bathes in these waters will find that certain ailments or disorders will be treated without the need for medical intervention, particularly when it comes to fatigue and poor blood circulation. In the past, the baths here were known as *Kogane-no-Yu* (the Golden Waters), although the waters were clear, and *Kodakara-no-Yu* (Child Waters), since they were not particularly hot and popular with women.

There are two types of waters to be enjoyed here: the waters that transform to a reddish-brown colour after the iron content has been oxidised, and clear waters known as Silver Water, or *Shirogane-no-Yu*. Situated along the Stone Steps, the source of the iconic clear waters of Ikaho Onsen can be found around 500 meters past the top of the steps. Covered by a clear casing near the public baths Ikaho Rotemburo, it was only discovered in recent times, despite providing water to the ancient bathhouses for centuries.

Address: 116-1 Ikahomachi Ikaho, Shibukawa 377-0102, Gunma Prefecture.

Hara Museum ARC

An annex of the Hara Museum of Contemporary Art in Shinagawa, Tokyo, the Hara Museum ARC features a fantastic collection of contemporary art from both domestic and international artists. The collections regularly rotate, offering a variety of themes to enjoy. In addition to its main facility, the museum also boasts the Kankei Pavilion where visitors can enjoy an awe-inspiring collection of traditional East Asian artworks. Due to its extensive grounds and countryside setting, the museum also features various permanent pieces scattered outside, including a giant replica of the Campbell's Soup Can by Andy Warhol.

Address: 2855-1 Kanai, Shibukawa 77-0027, Gunma Prefecture.

Mount Haruna (榛名山)

Stretching 1,449 meters above sea level, Mount Haruna-san is a dormant volcano which, along with Mount Akagi-yama and Amount Myogi-san, makes up the Three Famous Mountains of Gunma Prefecture. Situated at the top of the mountain is a crater lake, known as Lake Haruna, along with Ikaho, a hot spring town and various facilities for the comfort and enjoyment of visitors. In the winter, the lake freezes over and the ideal destination for ice fishing. During the warmer weather, visitors can hire boats and pedal boats or go fishing for the local wakasagi fish, a local delicacy served in many restaurants in the area.

The caldera on the mountain features an attraction referred to as Haruna Fuji, a cone-shaped and symmetrical projection which resembles Mount Fuji. There are several hiking trails around the mountain from the caldera and to various other areas, as well as a ropeway that takes visitors up to the top of Mount Haruna to take in the beautiful surrounding landscape.

The last time Mount Haruna erupted was around 550 CE. On the southeast side of the mountain sits the village of Shinto and Yoshioka town. The mountain's dramatic beauty has made it popular in modern culture, featuring within the manga series, *Initial D*, where it is known as Akina and is the location where the hero wins his first few races.

Address: Harunasanmachi, 370-3341, Gunma Prefecture.

Ikaho Town (伊香保町)

During the Sengoku Period, also known as the Warring States Period (1467 – 1603), the warlord Takeda Shingen (1521 – 1573) established the Ikaho Onsen in the foothills of Mount Haruna so that his soldiers could rest and heal themselves with the thermal waters nearby. Over time, the small encampment that housed his soldiers grew to become the thriving and vibrant town it is today.

The Stone Steps, a 300-meter-long series of stone stairs starts in the centre of the town, lined with traditional guesthouses, onsens, and souvenir stores, as it makes its way up to Ikaho Shrine. The staircase is old and has been renovated in recent years, although examples of the original stonework can be seen near the base of the slope at the Ishidan-no-Yu bathhouse.

There are several sites worth seeing along the Stone Stairs. The Villa of the Minister of the Kingdom of Hawaii can be found near the bottom of the stairs. Dating back to the Meiji Period (1868 – 1912), the restored building was constructed when Hawaii was still an independent country. Adjacent to the villa is a small museum which focuses on the relationships between Ikaho and Hawaii. Every year, the town celebrates this historic relationship by holding a Hawaiian festival along the Stone Steps with many events.

Ikaho Checkpoint stands next to the villa, a reconstruction of the original checkpoint which controlled the flow of traffic along the highway between Niigata and Gunma Prefectures centuries ago. In the Edo Period (1603 – 1868), these checkpoints were established in order to restrict travellers, who were required to produce permits to travel. Within the checkpoint is a small museum displaying weaponry, historical documents, hand-printed passes, and various other artefacts well worth checking out.

The centre of Ikaho town is located roughly halfway up the Stone Stairs, where the various restaurants, guesthouses, and stores are situated. Visitors can relax at one of the public baths, enjoy a meal, and browse the stores for souvenirs. A variety of traditional carnival games, such as shooting galleries, archery, and ring toss games, can be found in a few of the stores, where visitors can win prizes. In the evening, it isn't unusual to find guests wearing *yukata* as they stroll around the town, creating a wonderfully traditional and nostalgic atmosphere.

A little further up the Stone Stairs is the Ikaho Ropeway, which transports visitors up to the top of Mount Monokiki. An observation deck on the peak offers outstanding views over the surrounding area and should not be missed out on.

Ikaho Shrine stands at the top of the Stone Stairs, with a pathway that carries on to the Kajika Bridge. The iron rich reddish-brown waters that supply the town's onsens can be seen flowing beneath the bridge throughout the year, and for those who want to sample the water, there is a small drinking fountain alongside the road.

Address: Ikaho-machi, Shibukawa 377-0102, Gunma Prefecture.

Mizusawa Temple (水澤観音)

Founded over 1,300 years on the southwestern slopes of Mount Haruna, Mizusawa Temple is dedicated to Kannon, the Buddhist goddess of mercy and compassion. It has become almost the symbol for the town and is frequently visited by guests all over the country to come and offer the goddess respect and prayers. It is part of the Kanto Kannon Pilgrimage, which consists of 33 sites dedicated to the goddess.

The grounds of the temple consist of various buildings, including the principal hall of worship, a pagoda, and a bell house. Painted in a vivid red, the hexagonal pagoda is two-stories high, and adorned with mesmerising colourful and detailed carvings of animals. What makes the pagoda so unique, however, is that it boasts a rotating inner column; it is said that those who turn it three times will be blessed with good luck. An 11-faced statue of the thousand-armed goddess is enshrined here, but is never on display to the public.

Along the street below the temple are a series of restaurants famous for Mizusawa Udon, a local dish made with wheat noodles. Usually served cold with a soy or sesame sauce, they are regarded as one of the three famous udon noodles in Japan, alongside Sanuki Udon and Inaniwa Udon.

Address: 214 Ikahomachi-Mizusawa, Shibukawa 377-0103, Gunma Prefecture.

Ikaho Green Bokujo (伊香保グリーン牧場)

Located near Ikaho Onsen, the Ikaho Green Bokyjo is a farm themed amusement park boasting numerous workshops, rides, and attractions for all the family to enjoy as well as to get to know and experience farm life. Some of the attractions here include pony rides, horse-drawn coaches, a petting zoo, and a sheep dog show where real farm dogs guide a large herd of sheep, one of the largest demonstrations of its kind in the country.

The amusement park is a great experience for children of all ages as they can try milking and feeding cows before trying their hands at making butter. A miniature golf course, an archery range, BBQ areas, picnic grounds, a restaurant, and gift shops are just a few of the facilities available at Ikaho Green Bokujo.

Address: Shibukawa 377-0027, Gunma Prefecture.

Shinto Winery (榛東村ワイナリー)

Shinto Village is renowned for its production of grapes. Visitors can tour the winery, learn what makes the grapes in this area special, how wine is made and bottled, and sample some of its products.

Address: 1972-4 Yamakoda, Shinto-mura, Kitagunma-gun, Gunma Prefecture.

Funao Waterfall

The crystal-clear water from Mount Harunasan cascades over a 60meter high cliff, forming Funao Waterfall, one of the most serene and majestic falls in the prefecture. In the autumn, when the leaves transform from green to various shades of red, it is particularly inspiring.

Address: Kaminoda, Yoshioka-machi, Kitagunma-gun, Gunma Prefecture.

Mizusawa-dera (水澤寺)

Mizusawa-dera is a Buddhist temple founded by the officials of Kozuke Province during the Asuka Period (538 – 710) under the reign of Empress Suiko. Unfortunately, there are no records that date before the Edo Period to confirm this claim, nor any structures that date to this period.

The temple belongs to the Tendai sect of Buddhism and enshrines a bronze statue of the Juichimen Senju Kannon Bosatsu. The temple complex features numerous buildings and structures from various historical periods, boasting exquisite artworks and decorations. Surrounded by red maple and yellow gingko trees, the entire area is infused with a vibrant yet serene ambience.

Address: 214 Ikahomachi-Mizusawa, Shibukawa 377-0103, Gunma Prefecture.

Shibukawa Skyland Park

Shibukawa Skyland Park is a small amusement park featuring a variety of rides and attractions for all ages. Attractions include a Ferris Wheel, merry-go-round, rollercoasters, and bouncy-castle slides.

Address: 2843-3 Kanai, Shibukawa 377-0027, Gunma Prefecture.

Yumeji Takehisa Museum

Yumeji Takehisa (1884 – 1934) was a painter and poet, known for his *Nihonga* style paintings. Born in modern day Setouchi in Okayama Prefecture, a museum in Shibukawa was established to display many of his works and personal belongings, along with antiques from the period he lived in.

Address: 544-119 Ikaho, Ikahomachi, Shibukawa 377-0102, Gunma Prefecture.

Akagi Nature Park

Located near Akagikogen Hospital, the Akagi Nature Park is a public park where visitors can enjoy relaxing in beautiful surroundings. Situated at the base of Mount Akagi on its western side, the park has been designed that it reflects the best of nature throughout the year. During the summer, the park comes to life when thousands of flowers burst into bloom, whilst in the autumn turn to brilliantly vibrant colours. The park was designed to show the best of nature, and has provided the perfect home for many insects and plants native to the region. It is the perfect destination to enjoy walking, with plenty of benches for relaxing.

Address: 892 Akagimachi Minamiakagisan, Shibukawa 379-1113, Gunma Prefecture.

Restaurants

Mid-Range

Osawaya. 125-1 Mizusawa, Ikaho-machi, Shibukawa 377-0103, Gunma Prefecture. T: +81 279-72-3295. Cuisine: Japanese.
Banbino. 827-1 Arima, Shibukawa, Gunma Prefecture. T: +81 279-23-6778. Cuisine: Pizza.
Kinkodo. 3177-1 Handa, Shibukawa, Gunma Prefecture. T: +81 279-24-0101. Cuisine: Japanese.
Manyotei. 48-4 Ikahomachi Mizusawa, Shibukawa 377-0103, Gunma Prefecture. T: +81 279-72-3038. Cuisine: Japanese.

Budget Choices

Nagaishokudo. 4477-1 Kamishiroi, Shibukawa, Gunma Prefecture. T: +81 120-532-338. Cuisine: Japanese.
Shimizuya. 204 Ikahomachimizusawa, Shibukawa, Gunma Prefecture. T: +81 279-72-3020. Cuisine: Japanese.
Mimasuya. 221 Ikahomachimizusawa, Shibukawa 377-0103, Gunma Prefecture. T: +81 279-72-3018. Cuisine: Asian.
Ginzapateisuri Anteiku. 113-10 Ishihara, Shibukawa 377-0007, Gunma Prefecture. T: +81 279-25-8181. Cuisine: Japanese.

Accommodation

Four Stars

Moriaki Ryokan. 60 Ikahomachiikaho, Shibukawa 377-0102, Gunma Prefecture.

Three Stars

Pinon. 383 Ikahomachi Ikaho, Shibukawa 377-0102, Gunma Prefecture. T: 00 81 3-4510-3088.
Hotel Tenbo. 396-20 Ikaho, Ikahomachi, Shibukawa 377-0195, Gunma Prefecture.
Fukuichi. 8 Ko Ikaho, Ikahomachi, Shibukawa 377-0193, Gunma Prefecture.
Hotel Matsumotoro. 164 Ikahomachiikaho, Shibukawa 377-0102, Gunma Prefecture. T: 00 81 3-4540-9576.
Joshinnosato Hibikino. 403-125 Ikaho, Ikahomachi, Shibukawa 377-0102, Gunma Prefecture.
Seikanso. 557 Ikahomachi Ikaho, Shibukawa 377-0102, Gunma Prefecture.
Tsukagoshiya Shichibee. 175-1 Ikahomachi Ikaho, Shibukawa 377-0102, Gunma Prefecture.
Ichifuji Hotel. 557-12 Ikaho, Ikahocho, Shibukawa 377-0102, Gunma Prefecture.
Hotel Route Inn Shibukawa. 1186-1 Shibukawa, Shibukawa 377-0008, Gunma Prefecture.
Ryokan Fukuzen. 396-1 Ikahomachi Ikaho, Shibukawa 377-0102, Gunma Prefecture.
Yuzan no Sato Todoroki. 106 Ikahomachi Ikaho, Shibukawa 377-0102, Gunma Prefecture.

Chapter Three – Takasaki

Takasaki is often overlooked by other cities and tourist spots within Gunma Prefecture, but its laid-back atmosphere. A beautiful area for views, greenery and fresh air, the city is dotted with historical sites and cultural attractions, but still enjoys many of the comforts of a large Japanese city, making it well worth exploring.

With a population that hovers around 375,000, the city expands over an area of 459 square kilometres and is famous for being the homeplace of the Daruma dolls, which are said to represent Bodhidharma, and is a symbol of good luck.

During the Edo Period, the city was part of the Takasaki Domain, which was run by the Matsudaira Clan under the Tokugawa Shogunate. Due to the highway between Kyoto and Edo, Takasaki was able to flourish, with several post stations established within the city's modern-day borders.

Museum of Modern Art (群馬の森公園内)

Located within Gunma-no-Mori Prefectural Park, the Museum of Modern Art is housed within a building that resembles cubes stacked upon each other. Designed by Arata Isozaki, who won the Japanese Architectural Society Award, the museum houses a fantastic collection of Western-style paintings by artists such as Masao Tsuruoka, Kaoru Yamaguchi, Ichiro Fukuzawa, and Ichiro

Yuasa. In addition to modern art, there is an exhibition dedicated to traditional Japanese paintings, which also includes examples of calligraphy.

Address: 992-1 Watanuki-machi, Takasaki-shi, Gumma Prefecture.

Haruna Shrine (榛名神社)

Said to have been founded in 586 during the reign of Emperor Yomei, Haruna Shrine is a Shinto shrine dedicated to the gods of Water, Fire, and Agriculture. Situated on the slopes of Mount Haruna, one of the Three Famous Mountains of Gunma, it is believed that those who pray at the temple will receive good luck in marriage and business.

During the 14th century, the temple became affiliated with the Toeizan Kan'ei-ji Endon-in, a Tendai Buddhist temple in Ueno, Tokyo, but during the Meiji Restoration period, Buddhism and Shintoism were separated. As such, the Buddhist colours were removed from the temple and it became a purely Shinto temple once more.

The temple complex boasts numerous buildings and structures dating from various time periods. The main worship hall was constructed in 1806 and used for Buddhist worship; Shuanglong Gate was completed in 1855, named after the dragon sculpture and four rounded doors; The Kagura Library is a reconstruction of the original which dated back to 1764 and was designed in the Tang style with a gabled copper sheet roof.

Address: 849 Harunasan-machi, Takasaki-shi, Gunma Prefecture.

Takasaki Castle (高崎城)

First constructed in 1597, by Ii Naomasa (1561 – 1602), a general from the Sengoku Period, and regarded as one of the Four Guardians of the Tokugawa (the others being Honda Tadakatsu, Sakai Tadatsugu, and Sakakibara Yasumasa), Takasaki Castle sits within Joshi Park in the heart of the city.

Tokugawa Ieyasu ordered the construction of the castle, built on the foundations of Wada Castle, which had been built during the late Heian Period. Offering a strategic position on the junction that linked the Nakasendo (one of the five main transportation routes) and the Mikuni Kaido (an ancient highway), the castle was later relocated to its present-day location and renamed Takasaki Castle. After the Battle of Sekigahara in 1600, the Ii Clan were relocated to Omi Province (part of modern-day Shiga Province), and the castle passed through the hands of several *daimyo* clans including the Sakai, Ando, and various branches of the Matsudaira clan. In 1695, the Okochi Matsudaira clan took control of the castle, and, except for a few brief periods, remained in residence here until the end of the Edo Period.

Renovations and expansion projects were carried out throughout the centuries, with a major one taking place under the command of Ando Shigenobu. It lasted three generations over a total period of 77 years, which included a two-storey *yagura* (tower), and a three-storey *donjon*. In 1633, Tokugawa Tadanaga was exiled to Takasaki Castle by his brother, Shogun Tokugawa Iemitsu, to commit *seppuku* (ritual suicide). After the Meiji Restoration, many of the towers were subsequently sold and the moats filled in. Before the end of World War II, most of the buildings had been occupied by the Japanese Army.

Today, much of the original buildings are all lost, leaving only a few structures as a reminder of its past glory. In 1974, the city purchased the last remaining tower from its private owner and relocated to the Third Bailey. Six years later, the city also purchased the last surviving gate from the same owner and positioned it back on the grounds. The hall where Tokugawa Tadanaga committed *seppuku* was relocated on the grounds of a nearby Buddhist temple called Chosjo-ji.

Address: Joshi Park, Takasaki 370-0829, Gunma Prefecture.

Minowa Castle Ruins (箕輪城)

Minowa Castle was constructed in 1526 by Nagano Narimasa, whose family served the Uesugi Clan. In 1566, the castle was attacked by the Takeda Clan; inside, the garrison was led by Nagano's son, Narimori, and the famous samurai, Kamiizumi Nobutsuna. The majority of the castle fell during the siege, except for the part held by Kamiizumi Nobutsuna. Takeda Shingen, impressed by his abilities, asked him to join his forces, and when he declined, allowed Nobutsuna to leave unharmed. Minowa Castle was given to Naito Masatoyo, one of Takeda Shigen's generals, and would pass through the hands of several clans until 1590, when Ii Naomasa became lord. He would remain at Minowa Castle for only eight years before transferring to Takasaki Castle, leaving the original site to ruin.

Today, all that remains of the original castle are the moats, earthworks, and stone walls. It's size, 47 hectares or 116 acres, makes it one of the largest castle sites within Gunma Prefecture.

Address: Misatomachi Higashiakiya, Takasaki 370-3105, Gunma Prefecture.

Byakue Daikannon (高野山真言宗 慈眼院)

Also known as the White Robed Kannon, the gigantic statue of the Buddhist goddess of compassion and mercy can be seen from afar. Over 40 meters tall, it is one of the largest statues of the goddess within the country. Climbing to the top of the statue, visitors are afforded a magnificent view encompassing the entire city and beyond.

Address: 2710-1 Ishiharamachi, Takasaki 370-0864, Gunma Prefecture

Ishiharamachi Shopping Street

Situated just before the Byakue Daikannon statue, the Ishiharamachi Shopping Street is the ideal place to purchase souvenirs and the famous Daruma dolls. It has managed to retain a traditional feel, making it a wonderful place to wander and browse. For those who fancy trying something traditional, the market sells old-fashioned Japanese meals such as soba noodles and tempura.

Address: Ishiharamachi, Takasaki-shi 370-0864, Gunma Prefecture.

Shorinzan Darumaji Temple (少林山達磨寺)

If Takasaki is the home of Daruma dolls, then Shorinzan Darumaji Temple is the heart of the city. Many of the famous Daruma dolls are made at the temple, and the red-painted dolls can be found positioned throughout the complex. It is said that those who purchase one and make a wish will have it come true. A small museum dedicated to the dolls is located within the grounds of the complex. In January, the temple holds a grand festival where many Daruma dolls are ritually burnt. The complex features several buildings worth exploring as well as several trails that meander through the grounds.

Address: 296 Hanadakamachi, Takasaki 370-0868, Gunma Prefecture.

Susano Shrine (進雄神社)

Susano Shrine is a Shinto shrine popular with locals and said to be over 1,000 years old. A large wooden torii gate draped with a golden rope marks the entrance, and the flat pathway leads to the first buildings, surrounded by stone statues, and framed by beautiful greenery. Several historic halls and structures are scattered across the grounds, along with serene ponds and brightly painted bridges.

Address: 801 Shibasakimachi, Takasaki 370-0035, Gunma Prefecture.

Chokoju-ji Temple (白岩山長谷寺)

Chokoju-ji Temple is a small temple that enshrines the Buddhist goddess Kannon. The principal statue of the goddess is said to date from the late Heian Period but is not on display, although a replica from the Kamakura Period can be seen. The architecture is simple and elegant, boasting delicate carvings and decorations, whilst trees and flowers surround them, giving the entire complex a wonderfully invigorating atmosphere.

Address: 448, Shiraiwamachi, Takasaki, Gunma Prefecture.

Takasaki Tower Museum of Art (高崎市タワー美術館)

Located close to Takasaki Station, the Takasaki Tower Museum of Art displays an intriguing collection of contemporary and modern Japanese art, and offers several special exhibitions throughout the year.

Address: 3-23 Sakaecho, Takasaki Tower 21, 3& 4F, Takasaki 370-0841, Gunma Prefecture.

Gunma Prefectural Museum of History (群馬県立近代美術館)

Learn about the long and rich history of Gunma Prefecture from its prehistoric origins through ancient and medieval times to the modern era, with highly interesting exhibitions, models, and images on display. The Dongho Kofun Culture Exhibition Room features a fascinating exhibition on the region's ancient past, centring on excavated articles of Wenjin Kannonzan burial mound, allowing one to learn about the arts, crafts, and lifestyles of those from the Jomon Period. Other interesting exhibitions include the medieval period when Gunma Prefecture was locked within endless warfare, and the early modern period when the region started to prosper due to new industries.

Special exhibitions and workshops are held throughout the year at the museum, ideal for all ages.

Address: 992-1 Watanukimachi, Gunma no Mori, Takasaki 370-1207, Gunma Prefecture.

Restaurants

Mid-Range

Shinasoba Nakajima. 1190-4 Iizukamachi, Higashikanai Keneijutaku 1F, Takasaki 370-0069, Gunma Prefecture. T: +81 27-363-5161. Cuisine: Chinese.
Bikuya. 360 Harunasammachi, Takasaki 370-3341, Gunma Prefecture. T: +81 27-374-9255. Cuisine: Japanese.
Shangohonten. 1-10-24 Tonyamachi, Takasaki, Gunma Prefecture. T: +81 27-361-5269. Cuisine: International.
G.G.C. 1-28-2 Midoricho, Takasaki, Gunma Prefecture. T: +81 27-362-8887. Cuisine: International.
Ristorante Minerva. 1633 Egimachi, Takasaki 370-0046, Gunma Prefecture. T: +81 27-329-6021. Cuisine: Italian.
Restaurant Cafe Caro. 25 Renjakucho, Kotobuki Building, 1F, Takasaki 370-0826, Gunma Prefecture. T: +81 27-326-8688. Cuisine: European.
Bangkok Stamina En Nana. 70-50 Yashimacho, La Merce 1F, Takasaki 370-0849, Gunma Prefecture. T: +81 27-388-8222. Cuisine: Thai.
Moriokafe. Motomachi, Takasaki, Gunma Prefecture. T: +81 27-321-3643. Cuisine: Japanese.
Bishokuzairohasu. Kaminakaimachi, Takasaki 370-0851, Gunma Prefecture. T: +81 27-350-7684. Cuisine: Japanese.

Budget Choices

Donremiautoretto. Azumacho, Takasaki, Gunma Prefecture. T: +81 27-310-3828. Cuisine: Japanese.
Sobadokorokinoene. 37 Asahicho, Takasaki 370-0052, Gunma Prefecture. T: +81 27-322-5806. Cuisine: Japanese.
Yokohamaramen Shoyaegiten. 624-33 Egimachi, Takasaki 370-0046, Gunma Prefecture. T: +81 27-324-3321. Cuisine: Japanese.
Gatomarushie. 1-17-8 Higashikaizawamachi, Takasaki, Gunma Prefecture. T: +81 27-365-5630. Cuisine: Japanese.
Fujinoyaseika. 26-2 Ohashimachi, Takasaki, Gunma Prefecture. T: +81 27-322-7712. Cuisine: Japanese.
Pasutaru. 481 Nakaizumimachi, Takasaki, Gunma Prefecture. T: +81 27-372-8456. Cuisine: Italian.
Anrakutei Takasaki Kaizawa. 471-7 Kaizawamachi, Takasaki 370-0042, Gunma Prefecture. T: +81 27-364-2912. Cuisine: Indian.
Tsukijigindako. Asahicho, Takasaki, Gunma Prefecture. T: +81 27-330-3987. Cuisine: Japanese.

Accommodation

Three Stars

APA Hotel Takasaki Ekimae. 232-8 Yashimacho, Takasaki 370-0849, Gunma Prefecture. T: ++ 88 027-326-3111.
Takasaki Washington Hotel Plaza. 70 Yashimacho, Takasaki 370-0849, Gunma Prefecture.
Hotel 1-2-3 Takasaki. 2-23 Sakaecho, Takasaki 370-0841, Gunma Prefecture.
Dormy Inn Takasaki. 55-1 Aramachi, Takasaki 370-0831, Gunma Prefecture.
Hotel Sealuck Pal Takasaki. 556-1 Hamajirimachi, Takasaki 370-0005, Gunma Prefecture. T: 00 81 3-4579-3326.
Toyoko Inn Takasaki Eki Nishiguchi 2. 2-2 Tsurumicho, Takasaki 370-0848, Gunma Prefecture.
Hotel Coco Grand Takasaki. 3-5 Azumacho, Takasaki 370-0045, Gunma Prefecture.
Hotel Metropolitan Takasaki. 222 Yashimacho, Takasaki 370-0849, Gunma Prefecture.
Hotel Route Inn Takasakieki Nishiguchi. 128-4 Asahicho, Takasaki 370-0052, Gunma Prefecture.
Takasaki View Hotel. 70 Yanagawacho, Takasaki 370-0815, Gunma Prefecture. Website: https://www.viewhotels.co.jp/takasaki/
Central Hotel Takasaki. 263 Yashimacho, Takasaki 370-0849, Gunma Prefecture.

Two Stars

Business Hotel Suzuya. 22 Torimachi, Takasaki 370-0053, Gunma Prefecture.

Chapter Four - Kusatsu Area

    Located within Agatsuma District in the northwest of Gunma Prefecture, Kusatsu is a small town situated at the southeast base of Mount Kasatsu-Shirane-san. With a population hovering around 6,500 and spread over nearly 50 square kilometres, the town is famous for being one of the top onsen hot spring resorts within the prefecture.

    The town sits at an elevation of around 1,2000 meters above sea level, with the formant volcano, Mount Tengu, and Mount Motoshirane situated to the west. It is said that the hot springs at Kusatsu were first discovered by Prince Osu (Yamato Takeru) of the Yamato Dynasty, the 12th emperor of Japan, in the second century C.E, although there is no evidence to support this claim. The first record we have of the hot springs comes from the 12th century, folklore tells that Minamoto no Yoritomo, the founder and first shogun of the Kamakura shogunate, arrived here in 1193 as he chased after the fleeing Taira clan warriors, and bathed within the Yubatake.

    During the Sengoku Period, the town had become popular with wounded samurai. Correspondence between Tokugawa Ieyasu and Toyotomi Hideyoshi in 1595 tells how Hideyoshi recommends Kusatsu, but Ieyasu sent servants to fetch the water instead of going himself.

    The hot springs have continued to be a popular attraction throughout the centuries, and in 2014, they were voted as the best onsen within Japan for the 14th year running. Whilst the majority of attractions in and around Kusatsu are hot springs, the town does boast some other sites of interests and holds several festivals and special events throughout the year.

Kusatsu Onsen (草津温泉)

Said to have been founded by Prince Osu, also known as Yamato Takeru, Kusatsu Onsen has been used as a placed of healing and relaxation for well over a thousand years. Locals claim that its waters can heal anything but a broken heart. The waters are acidic and sulphurous, and not only used for bathing, but also heats the local primary and secondary schools, the local swimming pool, the welfare centre, houses, and the streets during winter.

Address: Kusatsu, Kusatsu-machi, Agatsuma-gun, Gumma Prefecture.

Manza Onsen (万座温泉)

Manza Onsen is a popular hot spring resort situated on the southern foot of Mount Kusatsu-Shirane, an active volcano, and one of the best-known mountains within the prefecture. Situated at an elevation of 1,800 meters above sea level, the onsen is nestled within beautiful secluded grounds and offers several baths for guests. In the past, it was one of the hardest onsens to reach, but modern development has made it accessible even in winter.

Each day, 5.4 million litres of hot water gushes out each day and contains the highest amounts of sulphur found in any onsen within Japan. It is referred to as *'the onsen that creates beautiful skin'*, and due to its milky-white waters, has long been popular with women, although for first-time visitors, the smell of sulphur can take a while to get used to.

In the spring, the flowers start blooming, and the mountain is laced with trails for guests to submerge themselves in all its natural beauty. The onsen resort itself is located within the Joshin-kogen National Park, popular with hikers. In the winter, several ski resorts open, attracting visitors from all over the world.

Address: Manza-Onsen, Tsumagoimura, Agatsuma-gun, Gumma Prefecture.

Yubatake (湯畑)

One of the most famous attractions in the Kusatu area, the Yubatake has become the symbol of the town. Meaning 'Hot Water Field' in Japanese, it is one of the principal sources of hot spring water, with an output of 5,000 litres every minute, making it one of the country's most productive hot springs.

The waters contain high levels of sulphur and reaches a temperature of 70°C when it comes to the surface before cooling a few degrees within the wooden conduits. From there, the water is distributed to various public baths and ryokans nearby. Around 100 name plates of famous people who have visited the onsen, such as Erwin Balz (a German doctor), Bruno Taut (an architect), Rikidozan (a pro wrestler), and Kakuei Tanaka (a Japanese prime minister). In the evening, the Yubatake is lit up, creating a splendid and romantic atmosphere.

Next door is the Netsunoya building, where visitors can experience the *yumomi*, the traditional ritual of cooling the hot spring water down using wooden paddles whilst singing folk songs. Performers usually have several visitors help participate in the show.

Address: Kusatsu-machi, Agatsuma-gun 377-1711, Gunma Prefecture.

Sainokawara Park (西の河原公園)

Sainokawara Park, situated only a short walk away from the centre of the Kusatsu onsen area, is spread over a valley where several outdoor hot spring sources are located. The stream that flows through the park varies in colour depending on its location – at times it looks greener, others more white – due to its mineral contents.

Pockets of water bubble up to the surface, forming pools and flowing down the valley before finally joining the main stream. A small waterfall fed by the hot water can also be found, along with the Sainokawara Rotemburo, a large outdoor bathhouse. Two outdoor baths, separated by gender, can hold up to 100 people each, with beautiful views that add to the experience. A number of trails lace the valley, making it popular with hikers.

Address: Sainokawara, Kusatsu-machi, Agatsuma-gun 377-1700, Gunma Prefecture.

Kusatsu Kokusai Ski Resort (草津国際スキー場)

In the winter, the steep slopes from Kusatsu Onsen to Mount Kusatsu Shirane are transformed into the Kusatsu Kobusai Ski Resort. Essential one long trail measuring eight kilometres, it is one of the longest continuous runs within the country. The top half of the run boasts several intermediate and advanced trails from the main route, whilst the bottom half features a broad field where beginners can learn comfortably.

In the summer, guests can enjoy a variety of activities such as mini golf, mountain and grass boarding, and hiking trails that meander around the mountain. A ropeway has been installed for guests who do not want to hike up to the top.

Address: Kusatsu-machi, Agatsuma-gun 377-1711, Gunma Prefecture.

Onioshidashi Volcanic Park (鬼押出し園)

Onioshidashi Volcanic Park was formed when Mount Asama-yama erupted in 1783, and once the lava cooled down, created immensely awe-inspiring natural works of art that continue to inspire today. In the past, locals would say it resembled the aftermath of a demon escaping the confines of earth. In the summer, a wide variety of flowers burst into bloom, creating a kaleidoscope of colours amongst the dark earth. Hiking trails meander around the park, passing several scenic spots, attractions, and a small temple.

Address: 1053 Kanbara, Tsumagoi-mura, Agatsuma-gun, Gunma Prefecture.

Mount Kusatsu Shirane (草津白根山)

The 2,160-meter-tall mountain is an active volcano, the summit of which features pyroclastic cones that overlap each other. Three crater lakes can be found here, the turquoise waters inviting to the eye, but its high acidic and sulphurous levels mean visitors cannot swim here. Visitors who wish to avoid the hike to the top can take the cable car, from Kusatsu Town. It is still possible to see snow on the mountain in June, making it a magical place to experience.

Address: Kusatsu-machi, Agatsuma-gun 377-1700, Gunma Prefecture.

Kusatsu Tropical Wonderland (草津熱帯圏)

Kusatsu Tropical Wonderland is a small zoo dedicated to tropical creatures such as crocodiles, lizards, snow monkeys, and many others. Visitors can interact with many of the animals, including the capybara and rabbits, and even enjoy a footbath where fish eat the dead skin off the feet, leaving them smooth and revitalised.

Address: 287 Kusatsu, Kusatsu-machi, Agatsuma-gun 377-1711, Gunma Prefecture.

Kosenji Temple (耕三寺)

Kosenji Temple is a Buddhist temple belonging to the Shingon Buddhist sect, originally constructed in 1200 by Kusatsu Ryuu Yumoto. Over the years, it has served as the residence for several historic figures, such as Emperor Hanazono, Kusatsu Yuji in Souken, Muneya, and Konoyu Ryoyama.

The temple complex features numerous important statues, buildings and structures dating from various historical periods. Notable buildings include the Bathing Dead Honour Tower, Yudokudo, Shakado, and the Murakoshi Fossil Monument.

Address: 446 Ko, Kusatsu, Kusatsu-machi, Agatsuma-gun 371-1711, Gunma Prefecture.

Shirane Shrine (白根神社)

Located a short walk from the centre of town, Shirane Shrine is a beautiful and elegant temple that sits in a quiet, secluded area. A long steep stone staircase leads up to the main shrine, a graceful wooden building that exudes a serene atmosphere. In the spring and summer, a variety of flowers bloom, making it the perfect destination to visit to appreciate Mother Nature.

Address: 538, Kusatsu, Kusatsu-machi, Agatsuma-gun, Gunma Prefecture.

Restaurants

Mid-Range

Matsumura Manju. 389 Kusatsu, Kusatsu-machi, Agatsuma-gun, Gunma Prefecture. T: +81 279-88-2042. Cuisine: Japanese.
Mikuniya. 386 Oaza Kusatsu, Kusatsu-machi, Agatsuma-gun 377-1771, Gunma Prefecture. T: +81 279-88-2134. Cuisine: Japanese.
Hakukotei. 376 Kusatsu, Kusatsu-machi, Agatsuma-gun, Gunma Prefecture. T: +81 279-88-2208. Cuisine: Japanese.

Sobadokoro Wahei. 486-2 Oaza-Kusatsu, Kusatsu-machi, Agatsuma-gun 377-1711, Gunma Prefecture. T: +81 279-89-1233. Cuisine: Asian.

Ristorante Al Rododendro. 557-11 Kusatsu, Kusatsu-machi, Agatsuma-gun 377-1711, Gunma Prefecture. T: +81 279-88-6150. Cuisine: Italian.

Ryuen. 116-2 Kusatsu, Kusatsu-machi, Agatsuma-gun 377-1711, Gunma Prefecture. T: +81 279-88-3777. Cuisine: Chinese.

Yakitori Shizuka. 396 Kusatsu, Kusatsu-machi, Agatsuma-gun 377-1711, Gunma Prefecture. T: +81 279-88-2364. Cuisine: Japanese.

Shino. 468 Kusatsu, Kusatsu-machi, Agatsuma-gun 377-1711, Gunma Prefecture. T: +81 279-88-5336. Cuisine: Japanese.

Accommodation

Four Stars

Kusatsu New Resort Hotel. 750 Kusatsu, Kusatsu-machi, Agatsuma-gun 377-1711, Gunma Prefecture. T: ++ 81 279-88-5111.

Naraya. 396 Kusatsu, Kusatsu-machi, Agatsuma-gun 377-1711, Gunma Prefecture.

Three Stars

Yubatake Soan. 118-1 Kusatsu, Kusatsu-machi, Agatsuma-gun 377-1711, Gunma Prefecture.

Kiyoshigekan. 280-4 Kusatsu, Kusatsu-machi, Agatsuma-gun 377-1711, Gunma Prefecture. Website: http://www.kusatsuspa.com/e/index.html

Hotel Ichii. 411 Kusatsu, Kusatsu-machi, Agatsuma-gun 377-1711, Gunma Prefecture.

Hotel Sakurai. 465-4 Kusatsu, Kusatsu-machi, Agatsuma-gun 377-1711, Gunma Prefecture.

Kusatsu Onsen Boun. 433 Kusatsu, Kusatsu-machi, Agatsuma-gun 377-1711, Gunma Prefecture. T: ++ 81 279-88-3251.

Hanaingen. 92 Kusatsu, Kusatsu-machi, Agatsuma-gun 377-1711, Gunma Prefecture.

Hotel Village. 618 Kusatsu, Nakazawa Village, Kusatsu-machi, Agatsuma-gun 377-1711, Gunma Prefecture.

Kusatsu Onsen Ryokan Yoshinoya. 95 Kusatsu, Kusatsu Onsen, Kusatsu-machi, Agatsuma-gun 377-1711, Gunma Prefecture. Website: http://yoshinoya932.com. T: ++ 81 3-4510-8932.

Kusatsu Hotel. 479 Kusatsu, Kusatsu-machi, Agatsuma-gun 377-1711, Gunma Prefecture.

Yumotokan. 366 Kusatsu, Kusatsu-machi, Agatsuma-gun 377-1711, Gunma Prefecture.

Mukashigokoronoyado Kanemidori. 162 Kusatsu, Kusatsu-machi, Agatsuma-gun 377-1711, Gunma Prefecture.

Two Stars

Kusatsu Onsen Eidaya. 464-285 Kusatsu, Kusatsu-machi, Agatsuma-gun 377-1711, Gunma Prefecture.

Hotel New Shichisei. 300 Kusatsu, Kusatsu-machi, Agatsuma-gun 377-1711, Gunma Prefecture.

Hotel Ohruri Kusatsu. 512-3 Kusatsu, Kusatsu-machi, Agatsuma-gun 377-1711, Gunma Prefecture.

Kirishimaya Ryokan. 541 Kusatsu, Kusatsu-machi, Agatsuma-gun 377-1711, Gunma Prefecture.

Hotel New Koyo. 464-34 Kusatsu, Kusatsu-machi, Agatsuma-gun 377-1711, Gunma Prefecture.

Pension Blue Bell. 464-424 Kusatsu, Kusatsu-machi, Agatsuma-gun 377-1711, Gunma Prefecture.

Hostels and Budget Accommodation

Kusatsukogen Youth Hostel. 464-1 Kusatsu, Kusatsu-machi, Agatsuma-gun 377-1711, Gunma Prefecture.

Chapter Five - Minakami

Situated at the foot of Mount Tanigawa-dake in the far north of Gunma Prefecture, Minakami is a famous onsen town, boasting dozens of hot spring resorts and outdoor activities to enjoy. Boasting a population of just under 20,000 and spread out over an area of 781 square kilometres, much of the town sits within the Joshin Etsu-kogen Highland National Park.

In addition to the numerous hot spring, including the famous Takaragawa Hot Spring, the largest mixed bath in Japan, there have been many companies established which offer a range of outdoor activities. These include bungee jumping, horseback riding, rafting, paragliding, snowmobiling, and many more.

In the past, the famous ancient highway, Mikuni Kaido, passed through Minakami, with nine post stations established. During the Sengoku Period, the town was fought over by rival clans including the Uesugi, Takeda, and Sanada clans. In the Edo Period, part of the town fell under the Numata Domain, whilst the rest was controlled directly by the Tokugawa shogunate.

Minakami Onsen (水上温泉)

The source of the waters which supply Minakami Onsen comes from the fast flowing Tonegawa River which rushes through between the two mountains within the Joshin Etsu-kogen Highland National Park. The onsen sits along the river valley close to the JR Minakami Station; in the past, it was known for its lively and energetic district, but these days it is much quieter and known for its relaxing atmosphere. The waters here are colourless and odourless, with a low concentration of minerals, making it ideal for sensitive skin.

Visitors can enjoy a range of indoor and outdoor baths, as well as horse-drawn carriage tours of the resort, and various attractions such as Suwakyo Gorge, are located nearby.

Address: Yubara, Minakami-machi, Tone-gun, Gumma Prefecture.

Takumi no Sato (道の駅たくみの里)

Surrounded by rice fields and apple orchards with mountains providing the perfect backdrop, Takumi no Sato is a splendid arts and crafts village. Visitors can wander around the village, popping into over two dozen workshops and stores, and browsing at the various traditional crafts produced here. Crafts produced at the village include making soba noodles, bamboo weaving, lacquer making, glass etching, painting, indigo dying, washi paper and many others. Some workshops offer hands-on experiences for visitors.

Address: Sukawa, Minakami-machi, Tone-gun 379-1418, Gunma Prefecture.

Mount Tanigawa (谷川岳)

One of Japan's 100 famous mountains, Mount Tanigawa stretches to a height of 1,977 meters above sea level. During the winter months, the mountain is crowned in thick white snow, which then feeds the Tone River when it starts melting in the spring. In the autumn, the slopes of the mountains and the valleys surrounding it blaze in rich red and gold tones as the leaves turn into different colours.

Mount Tanigawa is popular with hikers and mountain climbers, eager to explore and conquer its precarious slopes. The mountain boasts numerous trails for those who do not have much experience in hiking and mountain climbing, although for the more advanced hikers, there are a number of more difficult courses to take. For those who wish to enjoy the spectacular views but not the climb, the Tanigawadake Ropeway carries visitors to the top of the mountain.

The official hiking season for Mount Tanigawa runs between July and November, but the length of the trails largely depends how much snow has fallen. It takes around 2.5 hours from the base of the mountain to reach the upper ropeway station, and from this point it is another two hour hike to reach the summit. In the winter, the ropeway transports visitors to the Tanigawadake Tenjindaira Ski Resort, situated halfway up the mountain. Although it is a rather small ski resort, it boasts one of the longest ski seasons in the country, running from the middle of November all the way to May.

Address: Yubiso, Minakami-machi, Tone-gun 379-1728, Gunma Prefecture.

Tsukiyono Vidro Park (月夜野びーどろパーク)

Tsukiyono Vidro Park is one of the leading handmade glass factories within the country, producing wine glasses, vases, and many other crafts. Visitors can tour the factory, watching how the items are produced, as well as trying a glass-making class.

Address: 737-1 Gokan, Minakami-machi, Tone-gun, Gunma Prefecture.

Suwakyo Gorge (諏訪峡)

Suwakyo Gorge is a scenic spot close to Minakami Onsen. A promenade was constructed along the Tone River for visitors to enjoy the best views. The bridge sits at a height of 42 meters over the river, and is the only bridge bungy jumping spot in the country.

Address: Kohinata Minakami-machi, Tone-gun, Gunma Prefecture.

Tambara Lavender Park (たんばら)

Tambara Lavender Park is a popular ski resort named after the 50,000 lavender shrubs planted along the slopes. From spring to autumn, visitors can enjoy looking at the beautiful carpet of stunning flowers that covers the mountain slopes, or enjoy them from the ski lift. In the winter, the resort is ideal for those just starting to ski, or try out snowboarding.

Address: Tambara Kogen, Numata-shi, Gunma Prefecture.

Fukiware-no-taki Falls (吹割渓ならびに吹割瀑)

Fukiware-no-taki Falls is a charming waterfall featuring clear waters that cascade over a drop of seven meters high and 30 meters wide. Certainly one of the most popular attractions within

Gunma Prefecture, the rapid waters hitting the bottom of the river is an impressive sight. The views from the top are remarkable, and the beautiful surroundings are exquisite in the autumn when the leaves transform colours.

Address: 975 Tonemachiokkai,, Numata 378-0303, Gunma Prefecture.

Lake Akaya (赤谷湖)

Akaya Lake sits next to the famous Sarugakyou hot springs, and was formed after the creation of Aimata Dam. Originally, the hot springs sat alongside the riverbank, but after the dam was completed, they were completely submerged, but the source of the waters were preserved, which allowed a new resort to be established. As a result, many new onsens, hotels, inns, and restaurants have sprung up around the shores of Lake Akaya.

In 2005, it was proclaimed one of Japan's Selected 100 Damn Lakes and is a popular place for hiking, due to the various trails that meander through the woods surrounding the lake.

Address: Aimata, Minakami-machi, Tone-gun 379-1404, Gunma Prefecture.

Taineiji Temple (泉峯山 泰寧寺)

Taineiji Temple is a Buddhist temple in a secluded place surrounded by beautiful scenery. The grounds are slightly overgrown, but it adds to the serene atmosphere, surrounding visitors with a stillness that only comes with centuries of worship. Both the temple gate and the main hall are designated Important Cultural Properties, featuring exquisite decorations, and in the spring hundreds of hydrangea flowers burst into bloom.

Address: 98, Sukawa, Taisuiji, Minakami-machi, Tone-gun, Gunma Prefecture.

Restaurants

Mid-Range

Stone Stove Pizza la Biere. 681-3 Yubara Minakami-Machi, Minakami-machi, Tone-gun 379-1617, Gunma Prefecture. T: +81 278-72-2959. Cuisine: Italian.
Ikufudo Seinikuten. 814-1 Oana, Minakami-machi, Tone-gun 379-1611, Gunma Prefecture. T: +81 278-72-3574. Cuisine: German, Japanese.
Tsukinoyotei Gin no Tsuki. 1042 Mandokoro, Minakami-machi, Tone-gun, Gunma Prefecture. T: +81 278-62-1002. Cuisine: Japanese.
Umenomitsu. 780 Oana, Minakami-machi, Tone-gun 379-1727, Gunma Prefecture. T: +81 278-72-4573. Cuisine: International.
Ashima. 146 Yubara, Minakami-machi, Tone-gun, Gunma Prefecture. T: +81 278-72-3326. Cuisine: International.
Ayumi. 210 Sarugakyo Onsen, Minakami-machi, Tone-gun, Gunma Prefecture. T: +81 278-66-1313. Cuisine: Japanese.
Sukawa Chaya. 287-1 Sukawa Minakami-Machi, Minakami-machi, Tone-gun 379-1418, Gunma Prefecture. T: +81 278-64-0784. Cuisine: Japanese.

Asuka. 1022 Mandokoro, Minakami-machi, Tone-gun, Gunma Prefecture. T: +81 278-62-1310. Cuisine: Japanese.

Hachibe. 822-5 Sugawa, Minakami-machi, Tone-gun 379-1418, Gunma Prefecture. T: +81 278-64-0340. Cuisine: Japanese.

Accommodation

Four Stars

Hoshi Onsen Chojukan. 650 Nagai, Minakami-machi, Tone-gun 379-1401, Gunma Prefecture.

Bettei Senjuan. 614 Tanigawa, Minakami-machi, Tone-gun 379-1619, Gunma Prefecture.

Yado Kanzan. 430 Tanigawa, Minakami-machi, Tone-gun 379-1619, Gunma Prefecture.

Three Stars

Minakami Kogen Hotel 200. 6152-1 Fujiwara, Minakami-machi, Tone-gun 379-1721, Gunma Prefecture.

Micasa. 740 Yubara, Minakami-machi, Tone-gun 379-1617, Gunma Prefecture.

Sanazawanomori. 2537-2 Tsukiyono, Minakami-machi, Tone-gun 379-1313, Gunma Prefecture.

Syoubun. 277 Tsunago, Minakami-machi, Tone-gun 379-1725, Gunma Prefecture. Website: https://www.syoubun.com/

Hotel Ichiyotei. 701 Yubara, Minakami-machi, Tone-gun 379-1617, Gunma Prefecture.

Kamimoku Onsen Tatsumikan. 2052 Kamimoku, Minakami-machi, Tone-gun 379-1303, Gunma Prefecture. T: ++ 81 3-4540-9855. Website: http://www.tatsumikan.com/

Matsunoi Hotel. 551 Yubara, Minakami-machi, Tone-gun 379-1617, Gunma Prefecture.

Ryokan Tanigawa. 524-1 Tanigawa, Minakami-machi, Tone-gun 379-1619, Gunma Prefecture. Website: http://www.ryokan-tanigawa.com/

Hotel Sunbird. 4957 Fujiwara, Minakami-machi, Tone-gun 379-1721, Gunma Prefecture.

Minakamikan. 573 Obinata, Minakami-machi, Tone-gun 379-1612, Gunma Prefecture.

Shojuen. 1048 Sarugakyo Onsen, Minakami-machi, Tone-gun 379-1403, Gunma Prefecture.

Two Stars

Amanoya. 804 Yubara, Minakami-machi, Tone-gun 379-1617, Gunma Prefecture.

Chalet La Neige. 3831-7 Fujiwara, Minakami-machi, Tone-gun 379-1721, Gunma Prefecture. T: ++ 81 3-4540-3798. Website: http://la-neige.com

Oyado Matsubaya. 669 Obinata, Minakami-machi, Tone-gun 379-1612, Gunma Prefecture.

Pension Old String. 4985-25 Fujiwara, Minakami-machi, Tone-gun 379-1721, Gunma Prefecture.

Hostels and Budget Accommodation

Tanigawadake Raspberry Youth Hostel. 75-5 Tanigawa, Minakami-machi, Tone-gun 379-1619, Gunma Prefecture.

Yushima Auto Campground. 2004-31 Aimata, Minakami-machi, Tone-gun 379-1404, Gunma Prefecture.

I Love Backpackers. Kanosawa 172-1, Minakami, Minakami-machi, Tone-gun 379-1611, Gunma Prefecture.

Chapter Six – Nakanojo

Located in west-central Gunma Prefecture, Nakanojo is a town spread over 439 square kilometres with a population hovering around 17,000. It is surrounded by mountains dominating the skyline, with peaks over 1,000 meters high, with the Azuma River flowing through the centre of town, running from east to west. With 83% of the town made up of mountains and forests, it is a beautiful area for views, with lush greenery and fresh air.

Nakanojo is famous for its onsens, with much of its economy centred on tourism around these hot spring resorts. Shima Onsen is the most famous of these, and was selected as the first Nationally Certified Onsen in the country in 1954. Those who bathe here can be cured of up to 40,000 diseases and health issues according to local sources. The waters here contain sodium and calcium chloride, which is believed to have positive effects on skin issues, nerve pain, and digestive problems.

The city holds three main festivals during the year. Tori-oi Matsuri in winter, where large drums are beaten to drive away the birds and demons; Nakanojo Matsuri in August; and the Ise-machi Matsuri in September, where the famous Yagibushi folk dance is performed.

Shima Onsen (四万温泉)

Shima Onsen is perhaps the most famous onsen in the region. Situated along the Shima River Valley, it is surrounded by three distinctive towns; at the southern entrance to the valley is the lower town, known for its quiet atmosphere and its charming ryokan overlooking the river. The central town area is the heart of Shima Town, and features traditional narrow streets and arcades. The waters here are softer than others found elsewhere in Gunma Prefecture, and therefore ideal for visitors with skin complaints. The onsen is one of the oldest hot springs in the country, with over 40 distinct sources that supply the onsen resort and the ryokan in the area.

Address: Shima, Nakanojo-machi, Agatsuma-gun 377-0601, Gunma Prefecture.

Shima Seiryunoyu

Shima Seiryunoyu is a popular bathhouse situated in the lower town area and sitting along the Shimagawa River. It features the only outdoor bath in Shima, and the beautiful views overlooking the river and mountains adds to the relaxing atmosphere.

Address: 3830-1 Shima, Nakanojo-machi, Agatsuma-gun 377-0601, Gunma Prefecture.

Shima Yamaguchikan (四万やまぐち館)

This luxury ryokan is one of the largest and oldest within Shima, boasting a number of magnificent baths, including two outdoor baths situated along the river, and several private and indoor baths. Some baths are available to the public during the afternoon, whilst others are only for staying guests.

Address: Ko-3876-1 Shima, Nakanojo-machi, Agatsuma-gun 377-0601, Gunma Prefecture.

Sekizenkan (四万温泉 積善館)

Sekizenkan is one of the oldest ryokans within Shima, and said to be over 300 years old, and supposedly the inspiration for the bathhouses within the popular aminated film, *Spirited Away*. Indeed, one can almost imagine hoards of gods waiting inside standing on the iconic red bridge that stretches over the stream below. The bathhouse is extremely popular with bathers for its indoor baths that were fashioned in the Taisho Era, with large arched windows and tiled floors which is almost reminiscent of Roman bathhouses.

Address: 4236 Shima Ko, Nakanojo-machi, Agatsuma-gun 377-0601, Gunma Prefecture.

Gomusonoyu (御夢想之湯)

Known as the Hot Spring of Dreams, it is believed that Gomusonoyu was the original hot spring source. Local legends claim that the individual who discovered the hot springs was walking through the forest at night as they recited Buddhis sutras, led there in a dream by a mountain god. Today, the soft mineral-rich waters lead people from all over the world here to soak within the healing and relaxing waters.

Address: Shima Onsen, Nakanojo-machi, Agatsuma-gun 377-0601, Gunma Prefecture.

Hinatami Yakushido (日向見薬師堂)

Hinatami Yakushido is a small Buddhist temple situated next to Gomusonoyo which enshrines the Buddha of healing and medicine, Yakushi. Many onsens around the country honour the Buddha, since onsens are identified as places of healing. The main building was constructed during the Muromachi Period (1336 – 1573), and its thatched roof exudes a historic and dignified atmosphere.

Address: 4371 Shima, Nakanojo-machi, Agatsuma-gun 377-0601, Gunma Prefecture.

Okushimako Lake and (奥四万湖)

Okushimako Lake was formed by the Shimagawa Dam, fed by dozens of small streams that lace through the mountains that surround it. Located a short walk from Shima Onsen, the lake sits at a higher elevation than the rest of the town, and offers visitors the opportunity to relax and hike around the mountains and shoreline, with several waterfalls within the vicinity.

Address: Shima, Nakanojo-machi, Agatsuma-gun 377-0601, Gunma Prefecture.

Nozoriko Lake (野反湖)

The creation of Nozori Damn in 1953 (completed three years later) formed a beautiful reservoir lake known as Nazoriko Lake. It is popular in the summer with those seeking to cool off in the hot sun, and features easy trails that wind around the shoreline, as well as a small campsite on the far side.

Address: Iriyama, Nakanojo-machi, Agatsuma-gun 377-1701, Gunma Prefecture.

The Nakajo Museum of Folk History (ミュゼ中之条町歴史と民俗の博物館)

This small museum is dedicated to the preservation and education of the region's local history. It features an excellent array of artefacts, household objects, and traditional craft items that were used until modern times, along with a decent selection of weaponry.

Address: 947-1, Nakanojocho, Nakanojo-machi, Agatsuma-gun, Gunma Prefecture.

Restaurants

Mid-Range

Okinaya. 3982 Shima, Nakanojo-machi, Agatsuma-gun 377-0601, Gunma Prefecture. T: +81 279-64-2707. Cuisine: Japanese.

Tonkatsu Asunaro. 4231 Shima, Nakanojo-machi, Agatsuma-gun, Gunma Prefecture. T: +81 279-64-2159. Cuisine: Japanese.

Budget Choices

Moazanomuomukafe. 148-1 Isemachi, Nakanojo-machi, Agatsuma-gun 377-0423, Gunma Prefecture. T: +81 279-75-0611. Cuisine: International.

Yakimanju Shimamura. 4237-23 Shima, Nakanojo-machi, Agatsuma-gun 377-0601, Gunma Prefecture. T: +81 279-64-2735. Cuisine: Japanese.

Accommodation

Four Stars

Tsuruya. 4372-1 Shima, Nakanojo-machi, Agatsuma-gun 377-0601, Gunma Prefecture. T: ++ 81 3-4589-5617.

Shima Onsen Ryokan Yoshimoto. 4344-2 Shima, Shima Onsen, Nakanojo-machi, Agatsuma-gun 377-0601, Gunma Prefecture. T: ++ 81 3-4510-0314.

Shima Tamura. 4180 Shima, Nakanojo-machi, Agatsuma-gun 377-0601, Gunma Prefecture. T: ++ 81 279-64-2270.

Shima Yamaguchikan. Ko-3876-1 Shima, Nakanojo-machi, Agatsuma-gun 377-0601, Gunma Prefecture.

Shima Onsen Kashiwaya Ryokan. 3829 Shima, Nakanojo-machi, Agatsuma-gun 377-0601, Gunma Prefecture. Website: http://www.kashiwaya.org

Shima Grand Hotel. 4228 Shima, Nakanojo-machi, Agatsuma-gun 377-0601, Gunma Prefecture.

Toshimaya. 3887 Shima, Nakanojo-machi, Agatsuma-gun 377-0601, Gunma Prefecture.

Sekizenkan. 4236 Shima Ko, Nakanojo-machi, Agatsuma-gun 377-0601, Gunma Prefecture. T: ++ 81 279-64-2101. Website: http://www.sekizenkan.co.jp/

Three Stars

Sawatari Onsen Miyataya Ryokan. 2163-3 Kamisawatari, Nakanojo-machi, Agatsuma-gun 377-0541, Gunma Prefecture.

Hinatamikan. 4367-8 Shima Onsen, Nakanojo-machi, Agatsuma-gun 377-0601, Gunma Prefecture. T: ++ 81 3-4530-4081.

Hanamame. 21-1 Kosame, Nakanojo-machi, Agatsuma-gun 377-1704, Gunma Prefecture.

Hoshigaoka Sanso. 1539 Iriyama, Nakanojo-machi, Agatsuma-gun 377-1701, Gunma Prefecture.

Shojukan. 3895 Shima, Nakanojo-machi, Agatsuma-gun 377-0601, Gunma Prefecture.

Shiomaonsen Yunoyado Yamabato. 4358-11 Shima, Nakanojo-machi, Agatsuma-gun 377-0601, Gunma Prefecture.

Ayameya Ryokan. 4238-45 Shima, Nakanojo-machi, Agatsuma-gun 377-0601, Gunma Prefecture.

Ryokan Mikunien. 4362 Shima, Nakanojo-machi, Agatsuma-gun 377-0601, Gunma Prefecture.

Keisei no Yado Izumiya. 3981-1 Shima, Nakanojo-machi, Agatsuma-gun 377-0601, Gunma Prefecture.

Yumoto Shimakan. 3838 Shima, Nakanojo-machi, Agatsuma-gun 377-0601, Gunma Prefecture.

Chapter Seven – Tomioka

      Tomioka is a city situated in the southwest of Gunma Prefecture with a population of around 50,000 and covering an area of roughly 122.85 square kilometres. During the Edo Period, it formed part of the territory directly under the administration of the Tokugawa shogunate as part of the Kozuke Province. After the Meiji Restoration, it became Tomioka Town in 1889, and then later in 1954, it annexed the town of Ichinomiya and the villages of Ono, Nukabe, Takase, and Kuriowa. Four years later, the town was raised to city status. In 1960, it annexed the village of Nyuu and then the town of Myogi in 2006.

      The city's most famous attraction is the Tomioka Silk Mill and Related Sites, which includes Tajima Yahei Sericulture Farm, Takayama-sha Sericulture School and Arafune Cold Storage. Together, these form a World Heritage Site in 2014, attracting tourists from all over the world.

Tomioka Silk Mill (富岡製糸場)

      Founded in 1872, the Tomioka Silk Mill was the first modern silk factory in Japan, creating raw silk from silkworm cocoons. It was established with the aid of French specialists and the Japanese government to help improve the quality of silk in the country using modern machines and improving the working conditions for its employees. The establishment of the silk mill was part of the Meiji Period's government plan to modernize the country, thus catching up with the Western world.

In 2014, Tomioka Silk Mill was declared a World Heritage Site for its vital role in helping to establish Japanese silk as a major international commodity, and for its role in making the textile industry the most important industry within Japan. The textile industry would continue to play a significant role in Japan's modern era. Even Japan's major automobile manufacturers, such as Toyota and Nissan, have their roots within the Tomioka Silk Mill. A number of Nissan's engines originated from the automatic silk reeling machines, whilst Toyota first started out in the textile industry.

The location of the mill was vital to its success. Tomoika Town possessed good transportation infrastructure so that silk could be transported to Yokohama Port, as well as having fresh water and enough land to create a large factory. In addition, it boasted natural cold storage facilities so that the eggs of silkworms were able to be stored until required, in addition to having easy access to coal and other natural resources.

Today, the Tomioka Silk Mill consists of several well-preserved buildings. The main part of the factory is made up of three long brick buildings; the first of which is where the silkworm cocoons were reeled into silk reels. Visitors can head inside and see the machines used to do this in the 1980s just before the factory closed. The other two brick buildings are the warehouses where he silkworm cocoons were stored. The east warehouse is also open to the public, displaying an interesting exhibition, but the other buildings are closed off. Guided tours are available, along with audio tours in various languages.

Address: 1-1 Tomioka, Tomioka 370-2316, Gunma Prefecture.

Takayama-sha Sericulture School (高山社跡)

Located in Fujioka City near Tomioka Town, the Takayama-sha Sericulture School was established as a place where people from all over the country and worldwide could learn about sericulture, and the technology needed to raise silkworms to create raw silk. It obtained UNESCO World Heritage Status in 2014 along with Tomioka Silk Mill for its contribution of the silk industry's development in Japan.

The Takayama-sha Sericulture School was established by Takayama Chogoro, a former samurai who, in the later part of the feudal age, was able to perfect the seion-iku sericulture technique. This involves ensuring the humidity and temperature are balanced enough for silkworms by using a two-storied building with plenty of windows, fireplaces, and a raised roof for ventilation. As a result, Takayama Chogoro set the standard for modern sericulture techniques.

Guided tours are offered to visitors and start at the entrance gate. The school building was constructed in 1891 and was designed with the Tajima Yahei Sericulture Farm in Isesaki in mind. The first floor is always open to the public, and features fireplaces and a tatami room, and on quiet days the second floor can be explored, where the silkworms were looked after. Although there were several other buildings established on the grounds, many have either been torn down or are too badly damaged to explore, although there are plans to restore some of these to their original appearances in the early Meiji Period.

Address: 237 Takayama, Fujioka 375-0036, Gunma Prefecture.

Tajima Yahei Sericulture Farm (田島弥平旧宅)

Located in Isesaki City, the Tajima Yahei Sericulture Farm is a farmhouse residence constructed in 1863. It was created by Tajima Yahei who farmed silkworms and developed a ventilations system in order to grow high quality silkworm eggs. Numerous silkworm farmers visited the farm to study how to raise them, and in order to commemorate its contribution to Japan's modern silk industry, it was awarded UNESCO World Heritage status in 2014.

Tajima Yahei's ventilation system consisted of two-storied buildings with small raised roofs known as *yagura* positioned on top of the main roof. Because of this and the many windows positioned below it, it allows the silkworm eggs to be natural ventilated, allowing them to produce high quality silk. In the past, the farm consisted of two houses linked by a bridge on the second floor, but only the bridge and one house remain today.

Visitors can explore the gardens and view the building only; entering it is not permitted as descendants of Tajima Yahei still reside within it. Not far from the farm is an information centre with an interesting exhibition and movie on its history.

Address: 2243 Sakaishimamura, Isesaki 370-0134, Gunma Prefecture.

Arafune Cold Storage (荒船風穴)

Along with the Tomioka Silk Mill and the Takayama-shi Sericulture School, Arafune Cold Storage was awarded UNESCO World Heritage status in 2014 for its contribution to the country's modern silk industry. Located in the dense forested mountains close to Tomioka Town, the Arafune Cold Storage is the largest wind cave within the region, able to store a million trays of silkworm eggs. Wind passed through the crevices in the rock that fill with snow during the winter months, allowing it to stay cold throughout the year. Even in the height of summer, it remains just a few degrees aboe freezing.

Address: Minaminomaki, Shimonita-machi, Kanra-gun, Gunma Prefecture.

Gunma Safari Park (群馬サファリパーク)

Gunma Safari Park is one of two safari parks in Gunma Prefecture, housing a variety of animals including lions, tigers, and zebra. Visitors can either enter the safari park with their own car or take one of the park buses which takes guests around the different sections. Visitors can also feed some of the animals, including the lions, which adds a new dimension to the experience. In addition to the safari section, there is a small zoo for guests to explore, and an amusement park next door.

Address: 1 Okamoto, Tomioka 370-2321, Gunma Prefecture.

Gunma Natural History Museum (群馬県立自然史博物館)

Located in the northwest of Tomioka Town, the Gunma Natural History Museum is a fun, interesting museum that offers a fascinating collection to give a comprehensive overview on dinosaurs, local geology, and local natural and human history. The wide range of dinosaur skeletons are impressive enough to keep all ages intrigued.

Address: 1674-1 Kamikuroiwa, Tomioka 370-2345, Gunma Prefecture.

Myogi Shrine (妙義神社)

It is a steep climb up the mountain to reach Myogi Shrine, but this stunningly colourful temple is well worth the effort. After passing through a stone gate, a long stone staircase leads visitors to the main hall, with huge tree stumps lining the way. Some of the stairs are in poor condition, so care is needed here. A second gate sits at the top of the staircase, guarded by impressive stone statues of a red devil and a green devil, both dressed in tiger trousers. The main shrine sits beyond the gate, enshrining the gods of the mountain, with a smaller shrine behind it, dedicated to the *tengu*, legendary demons with wings.

According to the temple, Myogi Shrine was first established in 537 during the reign of Emperor Senka. However, it wasn't until the Edo Period that the shrine finally started to gain significance. It also served as the location for many samurai movies filmed during the 2000s.

Address: 6 Myogi, Myogi-mahi, Tomioka 379-0201, Gunma Prefecture.

Tomioka Suwa Shrine (諏訪神社)

Located a short distance from the Tomioka Silk Mill, a large impressive red torii gate marks the entrance to this small yet charming Shinto shrine, surrounded by shops and other commercial buildings. The elegance and exquisiteness of the wooden buildings gives it a pleasant atmosphere and an opportunity to explore a more local spiritual place.

Address: 1130 Tomioka, Tomioka 370-2316, Gunma Prefecture.

Restaurants

Mid-Range

Shinshuya. 51 Tomioka, Tomioka 370-2316, Gunma Prefecture. T: +81 274-63-2000. Cuisine: Japanese.
Shunno Zen Shirakaga. 343 Nakadakase, Tomioka 370-2333, Gunma Prefecture. T: +81 274-63-1401. Cuisine: Japanese.
Kyuko Shokudo. 1431 Tomioka, Tomioka, Gunma Prefecture. T: +81 274-62-0569. Cuisine: Japanese.
Hayami. 51 Tomioka, Tomioka 370-2316, Gunma Prefecture. T: +81 274-63-4039. Cuisine: Japanese.
Toentomioka. 1608-2 Tomioka, Tomioka, Gunma Prefecture. T: +81 274-62-3431. Cuisine: Chinese.
Tonkin. 1769-1 Ichinomiya, Tomioka, Gunma Prefecture. T: +81 274-63-4308. Cuisine: Japanese.
Girasole. 1757-1 Tomioka, Tomioka, Gunma Prefecture. T: +81 274-67-7000. Cuisine: Italian.
Nihao. 980-1 Ichinomiya, Tomioka, Gunma Prefecture. T: +81 274-64-3280. Cuisine: Chinese.

Accommodation

Myogi Green Hotel. 2678 Myogimachisugahara, Tomioka 379-0208, Gunma Prefecture.
Hotel Amuse Tomioka. 245-1 Tomioka, Tomioka 370-2316, Gunma Prefecture.

Chapter Eight – Katashina-mura

    Katashina-mura is a small village set in Tone District in northern Gunma Prefecture. Boasting a population that hovers around 4,500 and covering an area of 392 square kilometres, the village is set within the Oze National Park, the reason why visitors make their way here.

    Oze, situated on a plateau between 1,400 and 1,700 meters above sea level, is Japan's highest moor. Known for its marshlands, ponds, virgin beech trees, clusters of pine trees, and a variety of alpine flowers, it was designated a special natural monument of Japan in 1960, and stretches across the borders of Gunma, Fukushima, Tochigi, and Niigaa Prefectures.

    In addition to the Oze National Park, the region also features many onsens and ski resorts. Whilst there is no train station that stops at Katashina-mura, it is on the main highway route and easy to get to via car and local buses.

Oze National Park (尾瀬国立公園)

    Oze National Park, situated around 150 kilometres north of Tokyo, is an area consisting of open greenland that spans the borders of four prefectures. Its most famous feature is the Ozegahara Marshland and the Ozenuma Pond. The park also features a number of mountains , including the Aizu-Komagatake and Tashiroyama mountains.

The first national park to be opened within 20 years since the Kushiro Wetlands in 1987, Oze National Park is renowned for its alpine flowers in the spring, such as skunk cabbages, its autumn colours, and then for its thick blanket of snow which stretches across during the winter.

Numerous trails lace around the park, all of which are well maintained, with wide boardwalks which extends over Osegahara Marshland and around Ozenuma Pond. Experienced hikers will take around six to eight hours to follow the Hatomachitoge Trail to the Oshimizu Trail, passing the marshland and pond.

The Ozegahara Marshland is the most popular part of the park. Covering an area of around eight square kilometres, it features numerous small ponds with Mount Shibutsusan and Mount Hiuchigatake hovering over the horizon at the ends of the path. The Hatomachitoge Trail is around one kilometre long, making it popular with visitors. In the spring and summer, white skunk cabbages and the yellow alpine lilies grow throughout the park; in the autumn, the green grasses transform into vivid yellows and reds.

Ozenuma Pond is another highlight of the park, and can found east of Ozegahara Marshland, a 90-minute hike through the woods. A six-kilometre trail meanders around the pond and through the woods.

Address: Tokura, Katashina-mura, Tone-gun 378-0411, Gunma Prefecture.

Oze Iwakura (尾鷲岩倉)

Oze Iwakura is one of the largest ski resorts in the area, offering a range of 16 courses for beginners, intermediates, and advanced skiers and snowboarders. Ideal for all the family, it also offers day and night skiing, with the Milky Way Course having the longest run at 2,800 meters with an 18-degree slope.

Address: 2609 Tsuchiide, Katashina-mura, Tone-gun 378-0412, Gunma Prefecture.

Katashina Kogen (かたしな高原)

Located close to Oze Iwakura, Katashina Kogen is a skiers-only resort in Katashina-mura. The resort first opened in 1967, and has since then been a popular family-oriented ski resort, providing an excellent range of courses and facilities for all to enjoy.

Address: 2990 Koshimoto, Katashina-mura, Tone-gun 378-0413, Gunma Prefecture.

Nikko Shirasanesan Ropeway (日光白根山ロープウェイ)

Opening in 1950, the Nikko Shiranesan Ropeway is an aerial lift that transports passengers from within the Malnuma Kogen Ski Resort up Mount Nikko-Shirane, the tallest mountain within the Kanto region. In the winter, it mostly transports skiers, but is open to tourists throughout the entire year.

Address: 4658-58 Higashiogawa, Katashina-mura, Tone-gun 378-0414, Gunma Prefecture.

Tennozakura Tree (天王桜)

Said to be over 300 years old, the Tennozakura Tree is a magnificent cherry tree with a trunk circumference of 5.2 meters. Designated a Natural Monument of Gunma Prefecture, its dark pink blossoms burst into a fan-like shape, creating a spectacular sight.

Address: Hariyama, Katashina-mura, Tone-gun 378-0409, Gunma Prefecture.

Restaurants

Hatomachitoge Kyukeijo. 898-25 Tokura, Katashina-mura, Tone-gun 378-0411, Gunma Prefecture. T: +81 278-58-7311. Cuisine: Japanese.
Frying Pan. 1633-1 Higashiogawa, Katashina-mura, Tone-gun, Gunma Prefecture. T: +81 278-58-4038. Cuisine: Fusion.
Kamoshikamura Sobaya. 266-1 Tokura Katashina-Mura, Katashina-mura, Tone-gun 378-0411, Gunma Prefecture. T: +81 278-58-7047. Cuisine: Japanese.
Hishiya Sugenuma Eigyosho Yamagoya. 4655?16 Higashiogawa, Katashina-mura, Tone-gun, Gunma Prefecture. T: +81 278-58-2957. Cuisine: Japanese.
Kazuhachi. 1345-4 Higashikogawa, Katashina-mura, Tone-gun, Gunma Prefecture. T: +81 278-58-3428. Cuisine: Japanese.
Yoshimitei. 4078-17 Kamata, Katashina-mura, Tone-gun, Gunma Prefecture. T: +81 278-58-4313. Cuisine: Japanese.
Katashinaya. 4085 Kamada, Katashina-mura, Tone-gun, Gunma Prefecture. T: +81 278-25-4141. Cuisine: Japanese.

Accommodation

Umedaya Ryokan. 4073 Kamada, Katashina-mura, Tone-gun 378-0415, Gunma Prefecture.
Tsuchiide. 1958 Tsuchiide, Katashina-mura, Tone-gun 378-0412, Gunma Prefecture.
Oze Iwakura Resort Hotel. 2609 Tsuchiide, Katashina-mura, Tone-gun 378-0412, Gunma Prefecture.
Rokan Kiraku. 613 Tokura, Katashina-mura, Tone-gun 378-0411, Gunma Prefecture.
Yoshiyaso. 378-2 Hanasaku, Katashina-mura, Tone-gun 378-0408, Gunma Prefecture.
Oze Park Hotel. 982 Tokura, Katashina-mura, Tone-gun 378-0411, Gunma Prefecture.
Motoyu Sansou. 761 Tokura, Katashina-mura, Tone-gun 378-0411, Gunma Prefecture.

Chapter Nine - Maebashi

    The capital of Gunma Prefecture, the city of Maebashi is one of the most popular destinations within the region. Covering an area of almost 312 square kilometres and boasting a population of around 340,000, it is often referred to as the City of Water, Greenery, and Poets due its crystal-clear waters, its abundance of green areas, and that it is the birthplace of several renowned poets.

    Located at the foot of Mount Akagi, the city is also surrounded by Mount Myagi and Mount Haruna, with the Tone River, the second largest in Japan, and Hirose River flowing through it. In the winter, the *karakaze*, or dry wind, flows through Maebashi, sending the temperature plummeting. However, in the summer, the temperatures remain high since it is inland. Indeed, Maebashi is the farthest from the sea of all Japanese prefectural capitals.

    During the Nara Period 710 – 794), the area around modern-day Maebashi was called Umayabashi. It took its name from the fact that there was a bridge (*hashi*) which stretched across the Tone River, and a small refreshment house with a stable (*umaya*) that many travellers would use. In 1649, it was renamed Maebashi as it started to be redeveloped as a castle town and the administrative centre for the Maebashi Domain, directly under the control of the Tokugawa shogunate.

    Today, Maebashi is a beautiful city with numerous parks and green areas, a vibrant commercial and entertainment area, cultural activities to enjoy, and a range of historic sites to explore.

Gunma Flower Park (ぐんまフラワーパーク

Located on the southern side of Mount Akagi-yama, the Gunma Flower Park features a wide variety of flowers divided into several themed areas, such as the English Garden, and the Japanese garden. With a range of facilities for all the family, and plants that bloom in all seasons, this charming park can be enjoyed throughout the year.

Address: 2471-7 Kashiwagura-machi, Maebashi-shi, Gunma Prefecture.

Shikishima Park Rose Garden (敷島公園ばら園)

Shikishima Park Rose Garden was remodelled in 2008 and is now home to over 7,000 roses in 600 varieties. Between mid-May and early June, the garden hosts the Rose Garden Festival, where thousands arrive from all over the country to watch the beautiful plants lit up at night.

Address: 262 Shikishima-cho, Maebashi-shi, Gunma Prefecture.

Maebashi Castle (前橋城)

Originally constructed in the 15th century, Maebashi Castle has served as the residence of a branch of the Matsudaira clan, although several other clans took control of it over the following years.

In 1470, the Nagao Clan constructed a fortification on the banks of the Tone River. Named Ishikura Castle, it suffered serious damaged due to several floods. In 1560, Uesugi Kenshin took control of the castle and incorporated it into his own strongholds. Two years later, the Hojo and the Takeda clans recaptured it, but were not able to hold onto it. Uesugi Kenshin then gave the castle to Kitajo Takahiro, who then defected to the Hojo Clan two years later, then to the Takeda Clan in 1579.

In 1590, when Tokugawa Ieyasu seized control of the region, he initially gave the castle to Hiraiwa Chikayoshi. Eleven years later, however, Sakai Shigetada was installed as *daimyo*, and for the next seven generations, they completely rebuilt the castle on higher grounds, along with a three-storey *donjon*, and several baileys.

During the final years of the Edo Period, Maebashi started to develop further and prosper due to the silk trade, and since the lords had, by this time, relocated to a different castle, the Matsudaira Clan moved back in 1869. A new *donjon* was created, positioned further back due to flooding, and the outer walls were reconstructed on a zigzag line. Maebashi Castle was the last castle to be constructed in the Edo Period.

Today, the ruins of the castle are situated in a public park. Most of the buildings here were pulled down in 1871, but the main building continued to be used until 1928. Only one of the original gate have survived, although not in its original position.

Address: 1-1-1 Otemachi, Maebashi 371-0026, Gunma Prefecture.

Gunma Prefectural Government Building (群馬県庁舎)

Standing at a height of 154 meters, the 33-storey Gunma Prefectural Government Building is the tallest building within the prefecture. Visitors can ascend to the observation deck on the 32nd floor to enjoy the 360-degree panoramic views over the city, which are especially magnificent at night.

Address: 1-1-1 Otemachi, Maebashi 371-8570, Gunma Prefecture.

Akagi Shrine (赤城神社)

Situated on the shores of Lake Onuma, Akagi Shrine is nestled amongst the beautiful forests of Mount Akagi. It is long been popular with locals for the Seven-Five-Three Festival to perform exorcisms. The shrine also hosts various other festivals during the year; the two busiest times are at New Year's and in August.

The temple itself sits at an elevation of 1,300 meters above sea level, and is centuries old. One of the most unusual but beautiful traditions here features the koi fish. It is customary to make a wish to the koi fish, and then release them into the lake. If the wish comes true, one should return and dedicate more fish to the temple. The koi fish are considered sacred, and as such, highly respected by the locals.

The temple has been especially popular with women who pray to the goddess for easy childbirth and parenting. Visitors can also offer prayers to Akagi Daimyojin for success in business, studies, and driving.

Address: 4-2 Akagisan Fujimimachi, Maebashi 371-0101, Gunma Prefecture.

Lunar Park (前橋市中央児童遊園るなぱあく)

Lunar Park is a theme park suitable for children of all ages. It first opened to the public in 1954, and is one of the most popular theme parks in Japan. There are a wide range of rides and activities for children to enjoy, especially for the younger ones.

Address: 3-16-3 Otemachi, Maebashi 371-0026, Gunma Prefecture.

Rinkokaku

Rinkokaku is a wooden building constructed in 1884 and is designated as an important cultural property. It was designed by Motohiko Katori, the first governor of Gunma Prefecture, to serve as the first prefectural house. Many locals contributed to the cost of its construction, and Motohiko donated it to the city.

The Imperial family stayed at Rinkokaku whenever they visited Gunma Prefecture in 1893, 1902, and 1908. During World War II, Maebashi City Hall was damaged and so Rinkokaku served in its stead between 1945 and 1954.

Address: 3-15 Otemachi, Maebashi 371-0026, Gunma Prefecture.

Rtyukaiin Temple (龍海院)

Situated in downtown Maebashi, Rtyukaiin Temple enshrines the goddess Kannon, the Buddhist goddess of compassion and mercy. A dragon gate featuring two blue and red coloured deities serves as the entrance to the temple; inside, the complex features a number of beautiful buildings and structures, including a 13-tiered pagoda, incense vessel, a mantra prayer wheel, dragon fountain, and the principal hall of worship.

Address: 2-8-15 Kouncho, Maebashi 371-0025, Gunma Prefecture.

Arts Maebashi (アーツ前橋)

Located in the city centre, Arts Maebashi is a fantastic public art museum converted from commercial facilities. The museum is dedicated to supporting artistic and cultural activities, and to share them with the public. Hosting a range of ever-changing exhibitions, events, and workshops, Arts Maebashi is the cultural heart of the city.

Address: 5-1-16 Chiyodacho, Maebashi 371-0022, Gunma Prefecture.

Restaurants

Fine Dining

Komatsu. 4-5-4 Chiyodamachi, Maebashi 371-0022, Gunma Prefecture. T: +81 27-231-4140. Cuisine: Japanese.

Mid-Range

Harashimaya Sohonke. 2-5-20 Heiwacho, Maebashi, Gunma Prefecture. T: +81 27-231-2439. Cuisine: Japanese.
Katsuhisa Muan. 282-1 Kaminagaisomachi, Maebashi, Gunma Prefecture. T: +81 27-263-4129. Cuisine: Japanese.
El Viento. 1-3-12 Mikawacho, Maebashi, Gunma Prefecture. T: +81 27-220-5545. Cuisine: Spanish.
Sakufu. 1-9-7 Otemachi, Gunma Royal Hotel B1F, Maebashi 371-0026, Gunma Prefecture. T: +81 27-223-6111. Cuisine: Chinese.
Le Vin. 4-32-17 Minamicho, Terasawa Building. 1F, Maebashi 371-0805, Gunma Prefecture. T: +81 27-223-3311. Cuisine: French.
Sobahiro. 3-24-11 Odomomachi, Maebashi, Gunma Prefecture. T: +81 27-254-4187. Cuisine: Japanese.

Budget Choices

Shabushabu Dontei Maebashiiwagamiten. Iwagamimachi, Maebashi 371-0035, Gunma Prefecture. T: +81 27-210-1230. Cuisine: Japanese.
Koran. 4-2 Chiyodamachi, Maebashi 371-0022, Gunma Prefecture. T: +81 27-233-0351. Cuisine: Chinese.

Masajironopan. 1221-2 Rokkumachi, Maebashi, Gunma Prefecture. T: +81 27-265-6062. Cuisine: Greek.

Tanakaya. 3600-11 Sojamachisoja, Maebashi, Gunma Prefecture. T: +81 27-251-9480. Cuisine: Japanese.

Furaingugaden. 3-132-4 Bunkyocho, Maebashi 371-0801, Gunma Prefecture. T: +81 27-243-2622. Cuisine: International.

Kaisenryoridaishin. 413-4 Furuichimachi, Maebashi 371-0844, Gunma Prefecture. T: +81 27-252-0400. Cuisine: Japanese.

Kohikohi. 1-295-12 Nishikatakaimachi, Maebashi 371-0013, Gunma Prefecture. T: +81 27-234-5101. Cuisine: Japanese.

Panpukin. 950-6 Motosojamachi, Maebashi, Gunma Prefecture. T: +81 27-253-7023. Cuisine: Japanese.

Accommodation

Four Stars

Gunma Royal Hotel. 1-9-7 Otemachi, Maebashi 371-0026, Gunma Prefecture.

Three Stars

Comfort Hotel Maebashi. 2-18-14 Omotecho, Maebashi 371-0024, Gunma Prefecture.
Hotel Racine Shinmaebashi. 1-35-1 Furuichimachi, Maebashi 371-0844, Gunma Prefecture.
Business Hotel Luka. 1-19-22 Amagawa Oshimamachi, Maebashi 379-2154, Gunma Prefecture.
Bell's Inn Maebashi. 2-24-1 Omotecho, Maebashi 371-0024, Gunma Prefecture.
Toyoko Inn Maebashi Ekimae. 3-9-1 Minamicho, Maebashi 371-0805, Gunma Prefecture.
Hotel Sanderson. 3-12-2 Ishikuramachi, Maebashi 371-0841, Gunma Prefecture.
Maebashi Hotel. 2-16-1 Honcho, Maebashi 371-0023, Gunma Prefecture.
APA Hotel Maebashi Kita. 1-8-3 Mikawacho, Maebashi 371-0015, Gunma Prefecture.

Chapter Ten – Useful Phrases

Japanese can be a daunting language to learn but this guide includes a handy little phrasebook. This guide is to help you get your way around Gunma Prefecture, ask for directions, and how to say the names of the attractions in Japanese. This phrasebook is not designed to start you off at learning a new language comprehensively, but to help you on your trip.

English	Japanese	Romanization
Hello	こんにちは	Kon'nichiwa
Hello (polite)	もしもし	Moshimoshi!
I am	私は	Watashi wa
Thank you	ありがとうございました	Arigatōgozaimashita
You're welcome	どういたしまして	Dōitashimashite
Great	素敵	Suteki
Excuse me	すみません	Sumimasen
Please	お願いします	Onegaishimasu
It's nice to meet you	お会いできて光栄です	O ai dekite kōeidesu
How are you?	お元気ですか？	Ogenkidesuka?
Please let me introduce myself	私自身を紹介させてください	Watakushijishin o shōkai sa sete kudasai
My surname is…, my full name is…	私の姓は…、私のフルネームは…	Watashi no sei wa…, Watashi no furunēmu wa…
Goodbye	さようなら	Sayōnara
See you tomorrow	また明日ね	Mata ashitane
See you later	また後で	Mataatode
See you later	じゃあまたね	Jā matane
Good Morning	おはようございます	Ohayōgozaimasu
Good afternoon	午後	Gogo
Good evening	こんばんは	Konbanwa
Goodnight	おやすみ	Oyasumi
How do I get to the airport?	どうすれば空港に行くことができますか？	Dōsureba kūkō ni iku koto ga dekimasu ka?
How do I get to the train station?	列車駅にはどうやって行きますか？	Ressha-eki ni wa dō yatte ikimasu ka?

How long will it take?	どのくらい時間がかかりますか？	Dono kurai jikan ga kakarimasu ka?
Can we walk there?	私たちはそこに歩くことができる？	Watashitachi wa soko ni aruku koto ga dekiru?

Ordering Food and Drinks

Gunma Prefecture is full of wonders but indulging in authentic Japanese food is certainly a true highlight. A multitude of flavours and spices perfume the air and due to a love of food in Japanese culture, restaurants, cafes, and street food vendors can be found everywhere in the city.

Ordering Food

Please give me the menu	私にメニューを教えてください	Watashi ni menyū o oshietekudasai
Can you recommend some dishes please?	あなたはいくつかの料理をお勧めしますか？	Anata wa ikutsu ka no ryōri o o susume shimasu ka?
What would you like to order?	何を注文しますか？	Nani o chūmon shimasu ka?
Please clean the table	テーブルをきれいにしてください	Tēburu o kirei ni shite kudasai
I didn't order this	これは注文していません	Kore wa chūmon shite imasen
This dish is cold	この料理は寒い	Kono ryōri wa samui
Hot dog	ホットドッグ	Hottodoggu
Cheeseburger	チーズバーガー	Chīzubāgā
French fries	フライドポテト	Furaidopoteto
Crisps	クリスプ	Kurisupu
Onion rings	オニオンリング	Onionringu
Pizza	ピザ	Piza
Spaghetti Bolognese	スパゲティボロネーゼ	Supagetiboronēze
Lamb chops	ラムチョップ	Ramuchoppu
Roast beef	ローストビーフ	Rōsutobīfu

Sandwich	サンドイッチ	Sandoitchi
Salad	サラダ	Sarada
Breakfast	朝ごはん	Asa gohan
Lunch	昼食	Chūshoku
Dinner	ディナー	Dinā
Snack	間食	Kanshoku
Chopsticks	箸	Hashi
Spoon	スプーン	spoon
Knife	ナイフ	Naifu
Fork	フォーク	Fōku
Cup	カップ	Kappu
Plate	プレート	Purēto
Bowl	ボウル	Bōru
Napkin	ナプキン	Napukin

Ordering Drinks

English		
I would like….	したいのですが。	Shitai nodesuga
I will have this.	私はこれを持っていきます。	Watashi wa kore o motte ikimasu.
What would you like to drink?	飲み物は何にしますか？	Nomimono wa nani ni shimasu ka?
Oolong tea	ウーロン茶	Ūron cha
Green tea	緑茶	Ryokucha
Coffee	コーヒー	Kōhī
Black coffee	ブラックコーヒー	Burakkukōhī
Cream	クリーム	Kurīmu
Sugar	シュガー	Shugā
No sugar	砂糖なし	Satō nashi
Milk	牛乳	Gyūnyū
Juice	ジュース	Jūsu
Orange juice	オレンジジュース	Orenjijūsu
Apple juice	リンゴジュース	Ringojūsu

Pineapple juice	パイナップルジュース	Bainappurujūsu
Lemonade	レモネード	Remonēdo
Soft drinks	ソフトドリンク	Sofutodorinku
Cola	コーラ	Kōra
Water	水	Mizu
Mineral water	ミネラルウォーター	Mineraruu-ōtā
Ice water	氷水	Kōrimizu
Ice	アイス	Aisu
Beer	ビール	Bīru
Wine	ワイン	Wain
Red Wine	赤ワイン	Akawain
White wine	白ワイン	Shiro wain
Sparkling wine	スパークリングワイン	Supākuringuwain
Champagne	シャンパン	Shanpan
Wine list	ワインリスト	Wain risuto

Numbers

Number		
0	ぜろ、れい	Zero, rei
1	いち	Ichi
2	に	Ni
3	さん	San
4	よん、し	Yon, shi
5	ご	Go
6	ろく	Roku
7	しち、なな	Shichi, nana
8	はち	Hachi
9	きゅう、く	Kyû, ku
10	じゅう	Jû
11	じゅういち	Jû-ichi
12	じゅうに	Jû-ni
13	じゅうさん	Jû-san
14	じゅうよん、じゅうし	Jû-yon, jû-shi
15	じゅうご	Jû-go
16	じゅうろく	Jû-roku
17	じゅうしち、じゅうなな	Jû-shichi, jû-nana
18	じゅうはち	Jû-hachi
19	じゅうきゅう	Jû-kyû
20	にじゅう	Ni-jû
21	にじゅういち	Ni-jû-ichi
30	さんじゅう	San-jû
40	よんじゅう	Yon-jû
50	ごじゅう	Go-jû

60	ろくじゅう	Roku-jū
70	ななじゅう	Nana-jū
80	はちじゅう	Hachi-jū
90	きゅうじゅう	Kyû-jū
100	ひゃく	Hyaku
101	ひゃくいち	hyakuichi
102	ひゃくに	hyaku-ni
1000	せん	Sen
1001	せんいち	Senichi
10,000	まん	Man

Colours

White	白	Shiro
Blue	青	Ao
Yellow	黄	Ki
Green	緑	Midori
Red	赤	Aka
Orange	オレンジ	Orenji
Brown	褐色	Kasshoku
Black	黒	Kuro
Purple	紫の	Murasakino
Grey	グレー	Gurē

Shopping

How much is this?	これはいくらですか？	Kore wa ikuradesu ka?
Can you give me a discount?	私に割引をくれますか？	Watashi ni waribiki o kuremasu ka?
Can you lower the price?	あなたは価格を下げることができますか？	Anata wa kakaku o sageru koto ga dekimasu ka?
It's too expensive	これは高すぎる	Kore wa taka sugiru
I would like to return this	私はこれを返すと思います	Watashi wa kore o kaesu to omoimasu

| Do you take credit cards? | クレジットカードは使えますか？ | Kurejittokādo wa tsukaemasu ka |

Author Information

Founded in 2016, Beautiful World Escapes was established to provide reliable and up-to-date content in an authoritative manner but still draw out the magic of these locations.

Using a consistent format to provide clear information about its destinations and attractions, much of which may still be little known of, makes it easy to find what is needed. Each attraction has a genuine authenticity, giving the reader a feel for the colour and atmosphere, making each place unique. Combined with practical information, including hostels, restaurants, festivals, they also feature a handy phrasebook for getting your way around each destination and interacting with locals.

Come visit the website, Beautiful World Escapes, for more travel related guides and information.

BEAUTIFUL WORLD ESCAPES

WWW.BEAUTIFULWORLDESCAPES.COM

Made in the USA
Las Vegas, NV
17 April 2025